Wonderful Provence

Text **Nedjma Van Egmond**

Photographs **Jacques Debru**

Translation **id2m**

Editions OUEST-FRANCE

GARD
VAUCLUSE
BOUCHES-DU-RHÔNE
Alès
Nîmes
Avignon
Arles
Orange
Uzès
Beaucaire
Tarascon
Carpentras
Cavaillon
Salon-de-Provence
Aigues-Mortes
Stes-Maries-de-la-Mer
Port-St-Louis-du-Rhône
Martigues
Istres
Vitrolles
Étang de Berre
Étang de Vaccarès
PARC NATUREL RÉGIONAL DE CAMARGUE
LA CRAU
LES ALPILLES
GOLFE DU LION
0
10
20 km

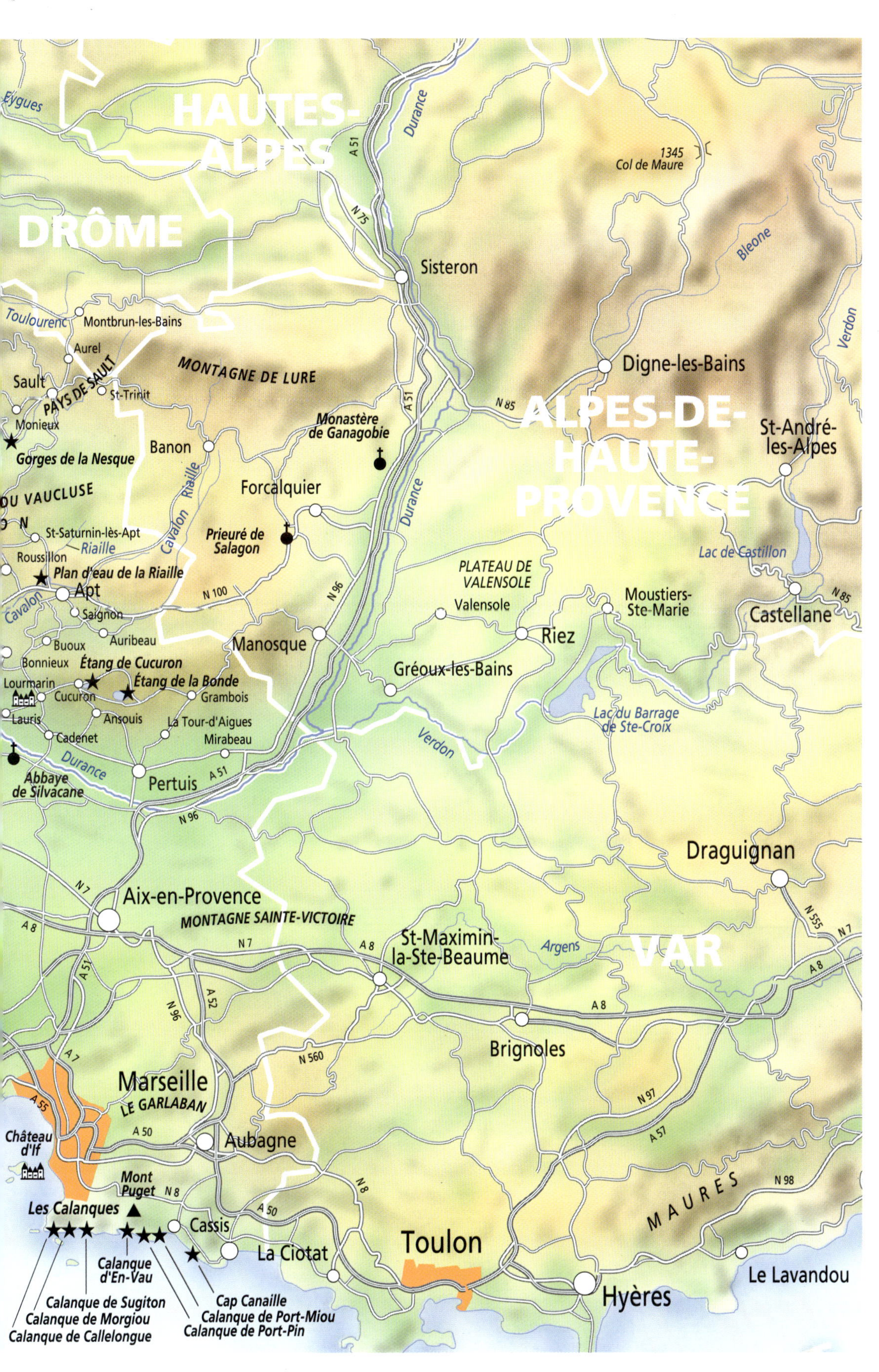

HAUTES-ALPES
DRÔME
ALPES-DE-HAUTE-PROVENCE
VAR
Eygues
Durance
A 51
N 75
1345
Col de Maure
Bleone
Sisteron
Toulourenc
Montbrun-les-Bains
Aurel
MONTAGNE DE LURE
Verdon
Digne-les-Bains
Sault
PAYS DE SAULT
St-Trinit
N 85
Monieux
Monastère de Ganagobie
St-André-les-Alpes
Gorges de la Nesque
Banon
Riaille
Forcalquier
DU VAUCLUSE
St-Saturnin-lès-Apt
Cavalon
Prieuré de Salagon
Riaille
Lac de Castillon
Roussillon
Plan d'eau de la Riaille
PLATEAU DE VALENSOLE
Apt
N 100
N 96
Moustiers-Ste-Marie
Castellane
Saignon
Valensole
Buoux
Auribeau
Manosque
Riez
Bonnieux
Étang de Cucuron
Gréoux-les-Bains
Lourmarin
Étang de la Bonde
Cucuron
Grambois
Lauris
Ansouis
Lac du Barrage de Ste-Croix
Cadenet
La Tour-d'Aigues
Mirabeau
Verdon
Abbaye de Silvacane
Pertuis
A 51
N 96
Draguignan
N 7
Aix-en-Provence
MONTAGNE SAINTE-VICTOIRE
N 555
A 8
N 7
A 8
St-Maximin-la-Ste-Beaume
Argens
A 51
N 96
A 52
A 8
Brignoles
A 7
N 560
Marseille
LE GARLABAN
A 55
N 97
Château d'If
A 50
Aubagne
A 57
Mont Puget
N 8
N 8
MAURES
N 98
Les Calanques
A 50
Cassis
La Ciotat
Toulon
Le Lavandou
Calanque d'En-Vau
Hyères
Calanque de Sugiton
Cap Canaille
Calanque de Morgiou
Calanque de Port-Miou
Calanque de Callelongue
Calanque de Port-Pin

An insight into Provence

Provence, one of France's most prized regions, is both unique and multifaceted. The administrative region is made up of six French *départements* - Bouches-du-Rhône, Alpes-Maritimes, Vaucluse, Var, Alpes and Alpes-de-Haute-Provence - but it would, of course, be impossible to do them all justice here.

Instead, this guide will focus on the very heart of the Midi, or South of France, as it is home to so many different treasures. Take, for example, the Camargue, a land of traditions with a harsh, wild beauty; the Gard area – admittedly a little outside the "official border" – with its Roman gems; the Alpilles, a land of legends; Marseille, the proud master of the open sea with its magical coastline; Luberon and its hilltop villages; Avignon, a major theatre both past and present; the *Enclave des Papes*, or Popes' enclave, part of the Vaucluse *département* which is completely enclosed within the Drôme *département*; the Aix and Haute-Provence areas, and finally Verdon, which boasts the deepest and most impressive gorge in Europe.

With its rivers, sea and vast dunes, jagged cliffs, scrubland abounding in thyme and rosemary, peaceful valleys, busy cities, quaint villages, and stony, green landscapes, Provence is a land of contrasts. With its late afternoon games of *pétanque* and refreshing *pastis*, its harbours exposed to the whistling wind and sing-song accents, its proud old-timers with their caps firmly planted on their heads, and its charming yet fiery damsels, Provence is renowned for its sometimes clichéd scenes but also its deep-rooted traditions.

It is also a land that has welcomed Corsican, Italian, Spanish, African and North African people, where skin colours blend into one, where names can be heard in a multitude of languages, and where influences convene whether they are linked to cuisine, traditions or history.

Many artists and writers, whether native to the region or late converts, have fallen immensely and unconditionally in love with the region and sung its praises in their texts and paintings. Paul Cézanne from Aix was drawn to Sainte-Victoire mountain; Marcel Pagnol from the Garlaban massif often used Marseille as a backdrop for his stories; Jean Giono from Manosque wrote about an "Imaginary South", and Henri Bosco and Albert Camus rest in peace in Lourmarin. There was also Frédéric Mistral, who led the revival of the Provençal language; Petrarch, the 14th-century Italian poet; René Char, the 20th-century French poet and resistance fighter, and Alphonse Daudet, the 19th-century French writer and playwright.

When visiting Provence you should allow yourself plenty of time. Time to discover it at your own pace, time to explore it off the beaten track, time to meet the people that live there, time to visit the place and then return, again and again, as there will always be something you have missed.

In the course of these fifteen or so itineraries, from the heart of Provence to the Provence of Cézanne and Giono via the *Vallis Clausa*, or Vaucluse, you will come across some real treasures. This travel guide is certainly not exhaustive but it contains some interesting ideas and helpful suggestions.

Provence is unique yet multifaceted. It is therefore up to you to find, and be won over by, the part of it that most resembles you…

A Provençal medley

Here is an informative yet entertaining guide to Provence.

Alpilles

This mountain range, a continuation of the Luberon massif, stretches over approximately 40 kilometres and boasts a harmonious blend of magical landscapes and charming villages.

Camargue

A land of harsh, wild beauty and the very heart of Provence. It is inextricably linked to the twice yearly *ferias* that are held from Arles to Nîmes and celebrate the art of bull fighting with *corridas*, or bull fights, *encierros*, or running with the bulls, and *courses camarguaises*, a game of chase where the bull is left unharmed.

Cicada

Souvenir shops abound in chirping ceramic cicadas, housed in pretty boxes. But we, of course, prefer these singing insects – which symbolise thoughtlessness in La Fontaine's fable *The Cicada and The Ant* – in the wild where they belong.

Fabric

Provençal fabric came to Europe from India in the 17th century. It was brought over by French East India Company boats and has remained characteristic of regional craftsmanship.

Festivals

The various music, drama, dance and cinema festivals have close links with local culture and hit the stage in summer from Avignon to La Roque-d'Anthéron, and from Aix to Marseille. It must be said that the warm and starry Provençal nights are just perfect for open-air shows.

Félibrige

This literary and cultural movement was founded in Vaucluse on 21 May 1854 by the Maillane-born poet Frédéric Mistral, among others. It included the *félibres*, or followers, Théodore Aubanel, Joseph Roumanille and Paul Giéra and its objective was to staunchly defend Provençal culture and language.

Gastronomy

Provence is home to *bouillabaisse* fish stew, *aïoli* garlic mayonnaise, *tian* vegetable bakes, tapenade, *pistou* soup, *anchoïade* anchovy paste, *papaline* chocolates and nougat. Whether sweet or savoury, flavours are of extreme importance in Provence.

Herbs

The name *Herbes de Provence*, or mixed herbs, alone is enough to get the taste buds going. Thyme – known locally as *farigoule* –, rosemary and savory from the scrubland all bring dishes to life here.

Inspiration

What region other than Provence has provided so much inspiration for artists from all fields? Its incredible colours provided Van Gogh and Cézanne with a vibrant palette, and its towns, villages and even its language have been celebrated by Bosco, Daudet, Zola and Giono.

Mistral

Not the poet but the cold northwest wind that rustles Provence for a considerable part of the year (from 90 days in Marseille to over 120 in the Rhône Valley). Its name comes from the Provençal word *mistrau*.

Luberon

This 60-kilometre mountain range stands against an incredibly clear sky. It is made up of rocky peaks, rolling landscapes, traditional villages with steep, cobbled streets, and very fashionable places. It is definitely worth the trip…

Market

There is not a village without a market here. Varying in size and speciality, they provide local people with fresh supplies and feature a delightful array of colours, flavours and perfumes. Fruits and vegetables, in particular, hold pride of place and are carefully arranged by stallholders with an incredible gift of the gab!

Pastis

The *pastaga*, as it is affectionately known by local people, or "little yellow", is an institution in these parts. This aniseed-flavoured alcoholic drink is enjoyed as an *apéritif* – for which there is no set time or duration! – in a specially-designed glass. Purists drink it neat with ice but it can also be served with various different cordials and consequently takes on different names – with a drop of grenadine it is a *tomate*, or tomato, a drop of mint cordial and it is a *perroquet*, or parrot, and a drop of barley water and it is a *mauresque*, or Moorish woman. Cheers!

Pétanque

"A game of pétanque is always fun, if you aim and miss, change your shot", went the famous French song... Originally from La Ciotat, *pétanque* can be played in teams of two (*doublette*) or three (*triplette*) and takes its name from the Occitan *pé tanco*, or "foot firmly on the ground".

Santon

Santon figurines (from the Provençal word *santoun* meaning little saint) decorate nativity scenes every Christmas in France. These painted terracotta figurines represent the Three Kings and the shepherds as well as popular Provençal characters, such as the fool, the grinder and the musician.

Smooth talking

Synonymous with the gift of the gab, this quality (or failing?!) is unavoidable in the South of France. The *tchatcheur* or smooth talker, a typically Southern French figure, is a braggart who happily recounts *galéjades*, funny stories that are very specific to local humour. To be told with *ze* accent of course!

Villages

Whether stationed on rocky headlands, carved into the rock face, perched on hillsides or nestling in valleys, Provençal villages have many facets... and are filled with character. No fewer than 18 of them in Provence have been awarded the *Plus beau village de France*, or One of the Most Beautiful Villages in France, label.

The very heart of Provence, set between land and sea

The Camargue, a land of traditions

The very heart and soul of Provence lies somewhere between the land, water and sky of the Camargue, a region combining beautiful, wild landscapes with a wealth of traditions that are very much alive.

Left
Close to 30,000 pink flamingos descend on the Camargue each summer.
Below
Grey is, together with Charnier and Scamandre, one of three lakes in Vauvert country.

The Camargue is first and foremost a stretch of Provençal and Languedocian land that runs from the river right down to the sea. This island, covering over 85,000 hectares, is hemmed in between the two branches of the Rhône River and the Mediterranean Sea. To the east (Bouches-du-Rhône side) there is the Grand Rhône, to the west (Gard side) the Petit Rhône, between the two there is the *Étang de Vaccarès* lake and to the south, the sea, with its 95-kilometre coastline from Grau-du-Roi to Fos-sur-Mer.

Listed as a Regional National Park since 1970, the Camargue features extremely diverse habitats (marshes and dunes combining salt and sand, lagoons and forests, rice fields and

Above The *gardians* are proud herdsmen that tend to their horses or bulls on horseback.
Below The *Courses camarguaises* tradition is still very much alive and these bull chasing events can been enjoyed throughout the region from April to September.

lakes) and is home to numerous emblematic species, including pink flamingos, white horses and black bulls. The former, with their majestic silhouettes and contented warbling, descend on the area in their thousands in the summer and the sight of them taking flight at dusk is really spectacular.

The Camargue is also associated with a few images that are more related to living traditions than populist clichés. For instance, you will no doubt see herdsmen (*gardians*), with their felt caps, neck scarves and western-style shirts and waistcoats, tending to their herds of horses or bulls (*manades*). Their brotherhood came into being in 1512 and French writer Marquis Folco de Baroncelli preserved their valued identity by creating the *Nacioun Gardiano* foundation in 1909 to lend his noble name to the community and promote its traditions.

You can experience these traditions first hand by attending one of the *courses camarguaises* (games to remove rosettes, strings and tassels from between the bull's horns),

held between April and September. Locals are always in high sprits at these events, which celebrate the quality of the bulls, the talent of the *raseteurs* (the white-clothed men chasing the bulls) and the beauty of the horses.

Below
The herdsmen, heirs of the Marquis Folco de Baroncelli, prepare for the *Abrivado* – taking the bulls from their fields to the bullrings.

Above
The *Croix de Camargue*, or Camargue Cross, created in 1924 at the request of the Marquis de Baroncelli, features the emblems of two key Camargue trades in days gone by – herdsman and fisherman.

Above

Seven of Arles' sites are World Heritage-listed, including the prestigious amphitheatre, which comes alive to the sound of the *Ferias de Pâques* and *Ferias du riz* twice a year, and the *Courses camarguaises* bull chases which include the *Cocarde d'or* event.

Right

Place de la République and its local figures – herdsmen and *Mireilles* (the heroine of Mistral's most famous work).

Arles, the little Rome of Gaul

Caesar established the "little Rome of Gaul" in 46 B.C. by stationing his legions here. Magnificent Arles – set at the crossroads between Crau (a semi-desert plateau of great ornithological interest), the Camargue and the Alpilles – reveals its treasures under a blazing sun. Roman and Romanesque monuments (including seven UNESCO World Heritage-listed sites) bear witness to two thousand years of history here. As a result, the amphitheatre, ancient theatre, thermal baths of Constantine, Saint-Trophime's cloister and various churches vie with one another to capture the attention of passers-by.

This privileged site is also blessed with an incredible light that enabled Vincent Van Gogh to produce some three hundred paintings during his 15-month stay here. Arles is not, however, a museum town but a lively

centre, set at the gates to the Camargue. It is a regular port of call for *aficionados* (bullfighting fanatics) travelling to the *corridas* and *novilladas* (young bull fights), held during the *ferias* at Easter and in September.

Above
Corridas, or bull fights, and herdsmen's festivals are important events in the Arles calendar.

Below Another example of Arles' outstanding architectural heritage is its ancient theatre (left). When the painter Vincent Van Gogh cut off part of his ear in December 1888, he was brought here, to the former Hôtel Dieu. Today it is home to a cultural centre bearing the name *Espace Van Gogh* (right).

Arles' *Fête du costume*, or costume festival

Many traditional festivals punctuate the Arles' calendar and the seasons in the Camargue. Art and traditions are inextricably linked and no town demonstrates this better than Arles. Every 1 July, its streets are adorned with colourful fabrics, silks, lace and satin that shimmer in the blazing sun. Some 500 locals take part in this costume procession and then attend the show, held on the ancient theatre's stage.

This festival dates back to 1903 and the *Festo Vierginenco* created by Frédéric Mistral, author of *Mireille*. To mark their entry into adulthood, young girls were invited to "collect their ribbons and dress". Eighteen young ladies took part in the very first festival and by the following year, this number had grown to 350! More than a century after its creation, the tradition is still very much alive...

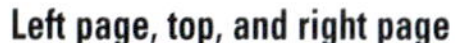

Left page, top, and right page

The beautiful *Mireilles* in their brightly coloured dresses parade on horseback with the *gardians*.

Bottom left

Eighteen young ladies took part in the first festival in 1903. Today, several hundred *Mireilles* parade through the town in the blazing sun with their parasols.

Saintes-Maries-de-la-Mer, a pilgrimage destination

It was on this shoreline that Mary Jacobe, Jesus' aunt, Mary Salome, mother of two of the apostles, and Sarah, their Egyptian servant, found refuge having been chased out of Palestine and put on a boat without oars or sails.

Every year, pilgrims pay homage to these saints. Celebrations take place in the months of May and October in honour of the two Saint Marys and on 24 May for Saint Sarah, or "Sarah the black", the venerated patron saint of the Roma people. The oblong town owes its fame to these frenzied rituals. Its old centre with its white façades, cobbled alleyways and imposing fortified church is also worth the detour as is its long sandy beach.

Above
One of the highlights of beautiful Saintes-Maries-de-la-Mer is its fortified church. It is open to the public and visitors can climb onto its roof, which has a superb view of the sea in the distance.

Left
Every 24 May, the Roma people pay homage to their patron saint, "Sarah the black".

The mediaeval town of Aigues-Mortes

Not far away, the great mediaeval town of Aigues-Mortes (or "dead water") dozes peacefully as if in a timeless age. In the 13th century, the small hamlet built in the heart of the marsh was only inhabited by a few fishermen and salt merchants. It belonged to Psalmody Abbey until French King Louis IX decided to build a town here with access to the Mediterranean Sea. Aigues-Mortes was built between 1246 and 1272, and its ramparts date from the early 14th century. The town also made a name for itself as a harbour.

Today, it is remarkably well preserved. Just look at Constance Tower, once a prison, and its almost perfectly quadrilateral 1,630-metre wall, both still fully intact! They captured the eye of Lawrence of Arabia back in 1908.

Below
Aigues-Mortes' ramparts, built in the early 14th century, have been remarkably preserved.

Right
Visitors are always eager to explore Constance Tower, which was once a prison.

The mediaeval festival

Oyez oyez! St. Louis is rising again... To honour the good king St. Louis – its founding father –, the peaceful town of Aigues-Mortes takes on a mediaeval atmosphere every summer. It remembers the time when the sovereign founded the town to gain access to the sea for his crusades.

For an entire weekend at the end of August, troubadours, knights, damsels, lords and minstrels get together in Aigues-Mortes for all kinds of revelry.

The beginning of the festival is generally marked by a torchlight procession, and the programme includes a mediaeval market, traditional jousting tournaments, parades and fireworks displays, much to the delight of locals and visitors.

Above
The mediaeval festival in full swing during an August weekend.
Left
To honour good king St. Louis, the founding father of Aigues-Mortes, knights and damsels parade through the town on horseback.

Le Grau-du-Roi, another facet of the Camargue

In 1927, Ernest Hemingway chose this resort for his honeymoon. Once a small fishing harbour, it has now grown in size but still promises many delights, such as the wonderful fisherman's waltz, the colourful fishing boats, the strolls along its narrow streets and the reassuring calm of Espiguette beach. This protected site, with its long stretch of fine sand, is a haven for daydreamers.

Close by, several other faces of the Camargue reveal themselves to visitors. There is another patch of wilderness in **Beauduc**, some 15 kilometres from Salin-de-Giraud. This site boasts flocks of pink flamingos and a very inviting beach. And there is also **Saint-Gilles**, a pilgrimage destination on the Way of St. James with a rich Romanesque heritage. Its 12th-century abbey church is World Heritage-listed. Explore it at your leisure.

Above
Espiguette lighthouse, a wonderfully preserved site that enjoys perpetual calm.

Below
The small fishing harbour that enchanted Ernest Hemingway has grown in size but retains its fishermen's waltz. Here, unloading the day's catch.

The Gard area and Ardèche

Left page
Vallon-Pont-d'Arc is set at the gates to the beautiful Ardèche gorge. It is quiet and unspoilt in winter but in summer becomes a meeting place for hundreds of colourful canoes.
Below
Nîmes' *Maison carrée* was built as a tribute to Caius and Lucius Caesar, grandsons of the emperor.

Nîmes, a historic yet modern town

Nîmes dates back to the 6th century B.C when the Celtic *Volques Arécomiques* tribe settled around a sacred spring, *Nemausus*, from which the city derives its name. The town grew and reached its peak under the reign of Augustus, when it was adorned with many majestic monuments. Nîmes' *Les Arènes*, or Roman amphitheatre, measuring 133 metres in length and 101 metres in width, is among the largest of the Gallo Roman period. It is also among the best preserved and

Left
The Sautadet waterfall, a lush corner of paradise that would be perfect for swimming and sunbathing after exploring the region's Roman architectural heritage. But be warned, bathing is forbidden here!

Right page
Above, Nîmes' remarkably preserved Roman amphitheatre, bursting with life during the *feria*.
Below, the *Jardins de la Fontaine* gardens.

Below
The *Carré d'art* contemporary art museum, which stands opposite the *Maison carrée*, was designed by architect Norman Foster in 1993 and links past and present.

can hold up to twenty thousand people! Just a short distance away, you will be astounded by the remarkable condition of the *Maison carrée*, or square temple, built as a tribute to Caius and Lucius Caesar, grandsons of the emperor.

Roman Nîmes also has much more to offer thanks to its innumerable influences and geographic location. It is as much Hispanic as Cévenole (of the Cévennes region), the Languedocian (of Languedoc region) or Provençal. Twice a year, festivals transform this town into a lively and passionate bullfighting capital. In contrast, not far away the Cévennes hinterland and Cèze Valley roll out their chestnut forests, green valleys, cool waterfalls and stone villages.

Nîmes also has a taste for fine things and offers visitors gourmet food with a regional flavour, for instance cod *brandade* and tapenade or olives and lamb, all washed down with a glass of Costières wine, whose vineyards stretch over 12,000 hectares.

Finally, this Town of Art and History also has a modern feel. Its *Carré d'art*, a contemporary art museum built in 1993 by architect Norman Foster, now harmoniously interacts with the venerable *Maison carrée* just opposite.

Above
The splendid *Château de Beaucaire*, which derives its name from *Belcaïre*, meaning beautiful stone (left). Sainte-Marthe Collegiate Church in Tarascon (right).

Below
Tarasque, the fearsome dragon and emblem of Tarascon, is released once a year for the festival of the same name.

Beaucaire, just a bridge away from Tarascon

Beaucaire, to the east of Nîmes in the Gard *département*, is separated from Provençal **Tarascon** by just 500 metres and a bridge. *Belcaïre* (beautiful stone) dates back to the late 11th century and its castle was built a century later. Many of its vestiges can still be seen today, for instance the polygonal tower, chapel and frescoes, dating from the Romanesque period. The town hall, Notre-Dame-des-Pommiers Church and Saint-Roman Abbey are also worth a visit, and from the necropolis, built on a terrace, there is a wonderful view of the lower Rhône valley. In the neighbouring town, the fearsome dragon with fiery breath and piercing eyes,

answering to the name of *Tarasque*, is released on the last Sunday in June for the town's annual festival. Do not miss Tarascon's beautiful castle of King René, a reminder of the d'Anjou family's reign, and the *Maison de Tartarin*, devoted to the hero created by French writer Alphonse Daudet.

Above
The *Château du Roi René* in Tarascon is remarkably well preserved. Its surviving tower, chapel and frescoes date from the Romanesque period.

Below
Its main courtyard and interior are open to visitors and serve as a reminder of the d'Anjou family's reign.

Above
The world's highest Roman aqueduct bridge runs for 273 metres and towers 49 metres above the water.

Right page
Following a visit to the museum that retraces the history of the bridge, many visitors take a dip in the Gardon River.

Pont du Gard, or bridge of the Gard, and 2,000 years of history

Nîmes' Roman aqueduct carried water some 50 kilometres from the sources of the Eure River into the town itself. The *Pont du Gard* bridge is its largest and most spectacular section. No one knows who designed the bridge but this symbol of Roman power is the highest aqueduct bridge of the Roman period, as is demonstrated by its breathtaking dimensions. Spanning the Gardon River, its three rows of arches run for 273 metres and tower 49 metres above the water. Several thousand men were involved in its construction, which lasted five years!

For it to be built, some 50,400 tons of local limestone were coated in lime mortar. Left to abandon in the 6th century, it was listed in 1840 by French dramatist and historian Prosper Mérimée, then inspector-general of French historic monuments. Modern-day visitors to this ancient marvel, set in an area of outstanding natural beauty, can also spend time in the contemporary visitors' centre, which retraces its history and hosts temporary exhibitions.

Uzès, the first duchy of France

While travelling through Uzège country, you must spend time in its capital, Uzès. Once home to a booming silk worm industry, it used to employ some two thousand people in the 18th century. Uzès, a bishopric from the 5th century to the French Revolution, was also the first duchy of France. The last Duke of Montmorency, formerly the first Duke of France, was decapitated after having opposed the king and so the title went to the Duke of Uzès. The castle still belongs to the d'Uzès family today and a flag is flown at the top of the building when they are in residence.

In addition to this ducal castle, which has a fabulous view from its Bermonde tower, other buildings are also worth visiting in this stone showcase. For instance, the 12th-century Fenestrelle tower, the Episcopal palace, Saint-Théodorit's Cathedral with its magnificent 17th-century organ, and the old bishop's palace, which today houses the town's museum with its beautiful collections of ancient ceramics. You will also enjoy passing under the town's porches and strolling through its streets to admire the impressive town houses and private residences. Of course, there are also

Top left

The 12th-century Fenestrelle tower dominates the skyline above Uzès.

Bottom left

The ducal castle – the pride of the town – still belongs to the d'Uzès family today. A flag is flown at the top of the castle when they are in residence.

Above Uzès is a harmonious blend of stone and greenery. Its centre conceals architectural treasures while the surrounding area abounds in plants and trees.

Below
One of the 2,000 *capitelles* – dry-stone huts emerging from the scrubland – in the Uzège area.

tiny squares with inviting pavement cafés and larger, more impressive squares, including *Place aux Herbes* with its picture-postcard market every Wednesday and Saturday. The very mild climate here yields delicious produce throughout the seasons, for example asparagus in spring, sweet fruits in summer, chestnuts and figs in autumn and truffles in winter.

Below
Visitors can enjoy a coffee under the arcades of *Place aux Herbes* before wandering through the Provençal market.

Truffles

Uzès, a Town of Art and History, is also renowned for its good fare and tasty local produce. The truffle naturally takes pride of place, particularly on the third Sunday of January during the truffle season. On this *Journée de la truffe*, or "day of the truffle", the locals celebrate this black diamond in all its splendour, and the festival is every bit as good as the ones in the *départements* of Drôme and Vaucluse! Food lovers and curious tourists descend on the town to watch dogs and pigs hunt truffles (photo below), meet the truffle growers and try out special dishes in the town's restaurants. But the highlight of the day is of course the Truffle Mass, celebrated in Uzès Cathedral. Once the service is over, the precious – and now blessed – truffles, are sold at auction.

Below

A demonstration of truffle hunting with a pig.

Above

The truffle is the star of the annual festival in Uzès. This black gold is blessed during a special ceremony and then sold at auction.

Ardèche, between Provence and Auvergne

If you head north, you will reach the *département* of Ardèche, nature's paradise. Admittedly, it is not strictly part of Provence but it would be a shame to exclude this corner of the Rhône-Alpes region between Auvergne and Provence that has both a continental and a Mediterranean climate. Beavers, eagles, oak trees, sculpted rock and chestnut groves share the limelight in this land, one third of which is covered in forest. Its volcanic sites bear witness to a distant "pyrotechnic" past... some 12 million years ago! Do not miss its magnificent gorge, dotted with colourful canoes and accessible via *Pont d'Arc*, a natural archway. According to the legend, this archway was formed when a jealous Sampzon lord wished for the return of his beautiful wife, who he had held prisoner. Prehistory lovers can also visit the *Musée régional d'Orgnac*, and the Vallon-Pont-d'Arc to see its exhibitions on the Chauvet and Huguenots Caves.

Above
Beautiful Pont Saint-Esprit is reflected in the waters of the majestic Rhône River.

Below
The Ardèche gorge can be explored from below, by canoe, or from above by car (or even by bike for the more intrepid visitors). The panoramic view is simply breathtaking.

The Alpilles and the surrounding area

Left page
The Alpilles mountain range stretches for forty kilometres.

Below
This glorious land with hilltop villages and wonderful legends is a patchwork of jagged peaks and sun-drenched valleys.

"A glorious and legendary vantage point"

This mountain range, a geological extension of the Luberon massif, stretches for forty or so kilometres, from the Durance Valley in Cavaillon to the Rhône in Tarascon. It holds jagged peaks – the highest of which (*Tour des Opies*) is 498 metres in altitude – and valleys bathed in sunlight, rustled by the wind and dotted with orchards, vines, olive and almond trees. And above all, it boasts a multitude of magical villages with dazzling light. Several artists found inspiration here, from Alphonse Daudet in Fontvieille to Vincent Van Gogh in Saint-Rémy.

Above

Eygalières is a peaceful village set at the foot of the Alpilles range. Do not miss Saint-Sixte Chapel and its small hermitage, located one kilometre to the east of the village.

Right page, bottom

Nostradamus fountain is named after the famous French physician and astrologer, who was born in Saint-Rémy. Known for his prophecies, Nostradamus also left behind many scientific and literary works (left). The *Plateau des Antiques*, at the edge of the town, should not be missed (right).

Frédéric Mistral, a child of the Alpilles, also began his *Mémoires et récits* with a reference to this mountain range: "As far back as I can remember, I have seen a range of mountains, to the south, whose hillocks, slopes, cliffs and valleys turn various shades of blue from morning to vespers, like huge waves. It is the Alpilles, a glorious and legendary vantage point."

Saint-Rémy, the small, peaceful town

Nostradamus was born here, Van Gogh spent the last year of his life here, and the *Félibrige* literary movement, led by Frédéric Mistral and Joseph Roumanille, met here. The charming old centre features beautiful town houses, fountains and a collegiate church. But it is the *Plateau des Antiques*, or antiquities plateau, at the foot of the magnificent Alpilles that catches everyone's eye. It is home to the vestiges of the ancient town of *Glanum*, destroyed by a barbarian invasion in the 3rd century. Visitors can still see traces of public baths, temples and the forum. There is also a triumphal arch and the *Mausolée des Jules*, or Julii family tomb, just opposite.

Above
The vestiges of the ancient town of *Glanum*, destroyed in the 3rd century.

Above
The remains of the former *Château des Baux*, set atop a rocky spur. It boasts spectacular panoramic views.
Below
Do not miss the house of the Montmorency family (left) and Saint-Vincent's Church (right) which dates, in part, from the 12th century.

Les Baux-de-Provence, the city of the lords

On the southern side of the Alpilles range, perched on a rocky spur, stands a village and its citadel. Les Baux-de-Provence takes its name from the Celtic word *bau*, meaning steep rock. The feudal lords who ruled over the village and its fiefs for five centuries were said to be descendants of the Three Wise Men. Their emblem was a 16-pointed star and their motto, *Au hasard Balthazar*, or "To fate, Balthazar". Left to fall into ruins by the feudal lords, Les Baux provided shelter for the Huguenots during the French Wars of Religion, before becoming a marquisate of the Grimaldi family of Monaco.

Today, this museum village is visited for its narrow streets, town houses, beautiful residences, churches, artists' workshops and breathtaking views. In fact, when the sky is clear (roughly 300 days a year), it is possible to admire Arles, Montmajour, the Camargue and La Crau. And do not forget to visit the remains of the castle.

For those of you who love extravagance, continue on to the *Cathédrale d'images*. These former quarries – once used to extract two different

types of rock (red bauxite and white limestone) – are the setting for a captivating sound and light show against an immense natural backdrop!

Above Les Baux-de-Provence takes its name from the Celtic word *bau*, meaning steep rock. The feudal lords who ruled over the village claimed to be descendants of the Three Wise Men.

Below: The surrounding countryside is worth the detour but visitors also enjoy wandering through the village's narrow streets.

Below
Montmajour boasts a blend of Romanesque, Gothic and Classical architecture.

Above
Montmajour Abbey should not be missed. Set between Arles and Fontvieille, it was built by Benedictine monks in the 10th century.

The Baux valley, Maussane, Fontvieille and Montmajour

Maussane is known for its delicious olive oil and beautiful village filled with fountains and vaulted houses. Not far away, there is also a lively *Musée des Santons*, or Santon museum, and *La Petite Provence du Paradou*, a miniature village that will delight all those interested in traditions.

In the former quarry village of **Fontvieille**, Saint-Pierre mill, built in 1814, was still in working order in 1915. It features a plaque with a quotation from Alphonse Daudet: "This corner of rock was a homeland for me and traces of it – whether people or places – can be found in almost all my books." Although it has been known as "Daudet's Mill" since 1935, it was not actually his mill! The writer never lived here, nor did he write his famous *Lettres* here. So why does it bear his name? Because it resembles the mills that Alphonse Daudet liked to describe in his texts. But do not let that stop you from visiting the place, as its small museum contains interesting manuscripts and portraits of the writer.

The history of Fontvieille was long associated with that of **Montmajour Abbey**, just four kilometres away. It is a wonderful blend of Romanesque, Gothic and Classical architecture, close to the town of Arles. Built by Benedictine monks in the 10th century, it stood on a rocky island surrounded by marshland, later turned into farmland. Today, the impressive abbey is only frequented by visitors.

Above The mill, which has been known as "Daudet's Mill" since 1935, contains manuscripts and portraits of the writer.

Below After Montmajour (left), you can explore the *Château de Montauban* in Fontvieille (right).

Above
The mediaeval village of Boulbon also has its castle… or at least some very interesting vestiges.

Below
The delightful view of Boulbon as you climb towards its summits.

Passing through Montagnette…

This hill, mostly covered in Aleppo pines, conceals a few pretty villages bathed in sunlight. **Barbentane**, once home to farmland and stone quarries, now makes for a peaceful stop over with its superbly-furnished Classical castle, dating from the 17th century. Medieval **Boulbon** also has its castle… and its customs. If you are passing through on 1 June for the Bottle Procession, be sure to get your bottle of wine blessed,

Above

Frigolet Abbey (left) and the Romanesque church (right) on Montagnette hill.

Below

The colourful 19th-century church reveals its treasures.

as it will then be bestowed with special virtues!

Finally, visit **Saint-Michel-de-Frigolet**, the Premonstratensian Abbey perched on Montagnette hill. The monastery features a Romanesque church and a richly-decorated 19th-century church, and is surrounded by beautiful scrubland overflowing with sweet-scented Provençal herbs.

Marseille and its superb coastline

Left page
Besides the popular legend of the sardine (!) that blocked the harbour, Marseille's *Vieux Port* is the very heart and soul of the Phocaean city.
Below
Calanque de Niolon, a real haven of peace.

Martigues and the Blue Coast

Like its namesake, "Provençal Venice" – an enclave on neighbouring Berre Lake – is home to numerous bridges and seven harbours. Its three districts, *Jonquières* in the south, *l'Ile* (or *Ile de Brescon*) in the centre and *Ferrières* in the north, are more like three mini-towns, and indeed they were, at one time, three independent towns. Martigues is known for its traditions, folklore and strong flavours. Its *poutargue*, or botargo, (pretentiously named "Martigues caviar") for example, is made of dried and cured mullet eggs.

The Blue Coast, which runs between Martigues and Marseille, is nothing short of magical with its *calanques*, or rocky inlets, sandy and pebble beaches, and steep jagged headlands. And it has something for everyone from *Calanque de Niolon* with its timeless fishing harbour to the quieter, calmer Ensuès-la-Redonne and Les Figuières.

Relative calm, that is, for the month of August!

If you are looking for livelier towns, head for Carry-le-Rouet, Sausset-les-Pins, La Couronne and Carro.

The railway line between Marseille and Miramas will soon be celebrating its one hundredth anniversary! The Blue Coast train is the ideal way to explore this corner of Provence, as it travels over bridges and past rocky inlets and seaside resorts, offering some breathtaking views.

Top
Martigues, the "Provençal Venice" and Saint-Sébastien canal.

Bottom
The beautiful beach of La Couronne is popular with locals at the weekend.

Above
Notre-Dame de la Garde, affectionately known as "Good Mother", jealously guards the port, the entire city of Marseille and the ocean beyond.

Marseille, "the great master of the sea"

Marseille, a city of myths and legends, does not open up easily to visitors and you will have to look past its many clichés before you can really appreciate its charm. The very name of the city has been associated with operetta heroes partial to recounting amusing *galéjades*, then with the warm portly characters in French writer and director Marcel Pagnol's trilogy, and finally with the gangsters who instilled fear in the city, once nicknamed Chicago. But Marseille has much more than this to offer thanks to its open-mindedness, its blend of cultures and its natural and architectural heritage, which is well worth exploring.

It is, in fact, a legend that holds the key to its creation. In the 6th century B.C., the Greeks of Phocaea landed on Marseille's shores. Gyptis, daughter of the Ligurian chieftain, was in search of a husband and she chose Protis, the Greek. At the same time as their union, an alliance was formed between the people of the land and those of the sea, and the town of *Massalia* was founded after the wedding.

After a very eventful history, Louis XIV decided to expand the

Left
Marseille's commercial port, still bustling with activity.

ancient city in 1666. Saint-Jean Fortress was extended and Saint-Nicolas Fortress was built. The city grew and its population increased through several waves of immigration – the French from Algeria arrived in 1962 followed by people from North Africa and Africa in the 1970s. Marseille does indeed seem to belong to those who arrive from the sea, as proclaimed by Franco-Swiss writer Blaise Cendrars. And its port was aptly named "one of the great masters of the sea" by French journalist Albert Londres.

Having been subject to chaotic urban planning, the city is gradually being returned to its former splendour, thanks to the restoration of its architectural heritage and the building of a tramway in the summer of 2007.

Above The Palais du Pharo, now a conference centre.

Left page
The breathtaking view from Notre Dame with the imposing silhouette of the New Major Cathedral towering over the old port.

Below Saint-Jean Fortress and Fanal Tower, also called the Round tower (left). The *Cité Radieuse*, or radiant city, designed by the architect Le Corbusier. It celebrated its 50th anniversary in 2005 (right).

Marseille has several fine examples of religious architecture, for instance Notre-Dame-de-la-Garde Basilica, affectionately known as *Bonne Mère*, or "Good Mother", by its inhabitants, who look to it for protection; the impressive New Major Cathedral, built in 1897, and Saint-Victor Abbey, a magnificent building that overlooks the *Vieux-Port*, or old port. The town's twenty museums also exhibit earthenware, paintings, archaeological collections and traditional folk art.

Above

After a small climb (!) you will reach Notre-Dame de la Garde, which reveals its rich and colourful decor.

Left

The New Major Cathedral, built between 1852 and 1893.

Finally, Marseille boasts 111 districts, each one a village in its own right with a very particular identity. These districts form a unique mosaic and include **Le Panier** district, set in the hills above the *Vieux-Port*, that has shed its terrible reputation and undergone a successful transformation. There is also **Belle-de-Mai** district, located behind Saint-Charles station. It seems to be stuck in a timeless age and yet looks to the future with its lively cultural centre, *La Friche*, or "Wasteland", housed in a former tobacco factory. And finally, there is the **L'Estaque** district, with its harbour and delightful narrow streets in the north of the city. It appealed to Cézanne, Braque and Dufy, and is sure to appeal to you too…

Above The flower market in Le Prado and the picturesque district of Le Panier, above the *Vieux-Port*.
Below *L'Estaque* district that appealed to Cézanne and Dufy.

Above
Take a boat from the *Vieux-Port* to explore the Le Frioul islands.

Below
The *Château d'If*, made famous by Alexandre Dumas' novel "The Count of Monte-Cristo".

The islands

The islands of Le Frioul and If can be reached by boat from the *Vieux-Port*. Le Frioul is a divers' paradise and If is famous for its castle, immortalised by French writer Alexandre Dumas as the former prison of Edmond Dantès, alias the Count of Monte-Cristo: "This fortress, which, for three hundred years, has sustained Marseille with its gloomy traditions... "

The wild beauty of the rocky inlets

Marseille may be a large city but half of its surface area (240 square kilometres) is made up of natural sites. Indeed, it is hard to believe that the pretty village of Les Goudes and Callelongue harbour are just on the edge of the city. From here, the southern coast stretches from Marseille to Cassis and you can admire its magical *calanques*, or rocky inlets, on foot or by boat. This 20 kilometre-stretch – part of a 57-kilometre sea front – is made up of steep limestone cliffs that plunge into the Mediterranean Sea. The most famous *calanques* include Sormiou and its Cosquer cave – revealed to the world between 1985 and 1991 –, Morgiou, Port-Miou, Sugiton and En-Vau. They are home to some 900 plant species, including Mediterranean sea lavender and crown vetch. It is not uncommon to catch a glimpse of seagulls and different tit species here, and if you are especially lucky you may even see the sky dotted with falcons or eagles.

Above
Those who have not explored the magical world of the *calanques* do not really know Marseille. This view embraces the *calanques* of Morgiou and Sugiton.

Below The *Calanque d'En-Vau*.

Cassis, in the shadow of Cap Canaille cliffs, and La Ciotat

To reach **Cassis** from Marseille, you will have a difficult choice on your hands. Should you go on foot along the coastal path or by car via La Gineste, the superb coastal road? The sea route no doubt offers the best view between the light-coloured cliffs and crystal-clear waters. When you arrive, you will be taken aback by the majestic Cap Canaille towering over the delightful little fishing harbour, the maze of narrow streets, steps and low houses in the old village, and the vast expanses of vineyards and olive trees in the surrounding area.

Some 12 kilometres away, there is another fishing harbour, **La Ciotat**. The ancient *Citharista* with its notable heritage appealed to French poet Lamartine who evoked its "harmonious beauty, found both in its features and in its lively inhabitants".

Left page, top
La Ciotat, known in ancient times as *Citharista*, is a delightful fishing harbour with an interesting architectural heritage.

Left page, bottom
The *pointus* – basic wooden boats – are very much part of the landscape in La Ciotat.

Above
Cassis harbour at nightfall.

Below
Cassis Bay and the *Route des Crêtes*, or cliff top road, gradually reveal all their treasures.

Vallis Clausa and its treasures

Avignon, the capital of Christendom

Avignon, famous throughout the world for its bridge and festival, indisputably deserves the praise it receives from its one and a half million visitors each year.

Left page The impressive Gothic-style *Palais des Papes* bears witness to the time when Avignon was the capital of Christendom. **Below** The view of the palace from *Ile de la Barthelasse* on the other side of the Rhône River.

This beautiful Vaucluse city was the capital of Christendom between 1305 and 1403, thus supplanting Rome. After the departure of the Supreme Pontiffs, it remained the property of the Holy See until it was returned to France during the French Revolution.

Clement V lay the foundations for its transformation, followed by John XXII, Benedict XII and all their successors. In total, seven

Above
A vast circuit enables you to follow in the footsteps of various Supreme Pontiffs. Here, the *Salle du Consistoire*, or Consistory Hall.

Below
The Refectory and the Pope's Chamber with magnificent paintings.

popes and two antipopes held office here. Their presence on the banks of the Rhône River marked an era of architectural, demographic, economic and cultural change, and many of the outstanding treasures of this period still remain today.

The pride of the city is undoubtedly its impressive and mysterious *Palais des Papes*, or Popes' Palace. Built in "only" 20 years, it is one of the largest Gothic monuments in the world and rolls out its chapels, rooms and innumerable staircases over an incredible 15,000 square metres! It features a multitude of treasures, including the *Chambre du Cerf*, or Stag Room, with its hunting scenes, Saint-Martial Chapel with its Giovannetti frescoes, and the earthenware of the *Chambre du Pape*, or Pope's Chamber. Do not forget to climb up to the *Terrasse des Hauts-Dignitaires*, or The Great Dignitaries' Terraces, to get a glimpse of the breathtaking view.

Above
Pope Gregory XI, one of the seven popes and two antipopes that resided in Avignon, held office between 1370 and 1378.

Below
Rocher des Doms gardens, a haven of green, backs onto Notre-Dame-des-Doms Cathedral.

Above
Known as *Pont Saint-Bénézet* to the locals, the *Pont d'Avignon* is famous throughout the world for its song and missing arches.

Below
The pond in *Rocher des Doms* gardens, a favourite with ducks (left). Close up of the bishop's chair in Notre-Dame-des-Doms Cathedral.

Several bridges, leading to the neighbouring Gard *département*, straddle the Rhône just a few metres from the palace but *the* Pont d'Avignon is in fact Saint-Bénezet bridge. This particular bridge does not lead anywhere any more, as over the centuries most of its arches have collapsed or been swept away by flooding. And it is exactly for this reason that the bridge, reputedly

built by an Ardèche shepherd, is so famous…

Visitors like to wander along it, never reaching the opposite bank, humming the famous "On the Bridge of Avignon" tune quietly to themselves. Note, however, that contrary to the title of the song, it was not on the bridge that people used to dance but rather under it!

Your tour of the City of the Popes does not end here however. There is still plenty to see between the city itself, Notre-Dame-des-Doms – its only example of Romanesque architecture, watched over by a gilded Virgin – and the nearby park, a prehistoric site and the birthplace of the city. There is also an abundance of museums to suit all tastes. Van Gogh, Manet and Daumier can be found in the *Fondation Angladon-Dubrujeaud*, decorative arts in the *Musée Louis-Vouland*, Italian traditional folk art in *Le Petit-Palais*, and contemporary masterpieces, or the

Above
The *Musée Angladon-Dubrujeaud*. This former private residence features period furniture and collections from arts patron Jacques Doucet. Its many treasures include works by Modigliani, Manet and Van Gogh.

Below
Hôtel de la Monnaie opposite Avignon's Popes' Palace. For a long time, it was home to the *Conservatoire*, or academy of music.

Opposite
The *Festival d'Avignon* – created in 1947 as a "week of art" – is one of the world's leading theatre festivals and it brings the town to life every July.

Below
The *Maison Jean Vilar*, opened in honour of the festival, displays legendary costumes, such as the one worn by French actor Gérard Philipe, who played *Rodrigue* in Corneille's *Le Cid*.

Collection Lambert, in the *Hôtel Caumont*.

It would be impossible to end this dazzling tour without mentioning the theatre festival that has earned Avignon a reputation throughout the world. Since Séte-born Jean Vilar chose the city as the setting for his theatre week in September 1947, it has become a centre for all living arts. Some 900 performances, including classical and contemporary plays, comedy and dance, circus acts and puppet shows, are held here every July from early morning to late into the night!

Above
On the other side of the Rhône River, the delightful mediaeval town of Villeneuve-lèz-Avignon and its beautiful Saint-André Fortress.

Below
Philip the Fair's tower, one of the town's landmarks.

Villeneuve, the twin sister

Villeneuve is located in another *département*, the Gard, and in another region, *Languedoc-Roussillon*, but it is like a twin sister to Avignon, as the two are separated by just a bridge and a few kilometres. Each town can see the other reflected in the pretty mirror of the Rhône River.

When the King of France besieged Avignon in 1226, the Abbot of Saint-André signed a treaty that made Louis VIII joint lord of the city. This act was confirmed by Philip IV of France seventy years later.

Peaceful Villeneuve still features numerous palaces, convents and fortresses, and with its calm narrow streets and stone façades, it is well worth crossing the river to explore. Its many treasures include Saint-André Abbey and fortress, which has a wonderful view from between its twin towers, and also *Tour Philippe-le-Bel*, or Philip the Fair's tower, and the Charterhouse of Val-de-Bénédiction. Still the largest charterhouse in Europe, it is today home to the *Centre national d'écritures du spectacle* for aspiring playwrights.

The Luberon, an enchanting old mountain

"An old mountain worn by time, which has experienced the rain, wind, snow and that mysterious friction between the sky and land that has charged the shapes of the earth to form special sites."

Left page
The beautiful village of Lacoste is dominated by the remains of the castle once owned by the Marquis de Sade. Today it is the property of French designer Pierre Cardin.
Below
The sleepy village of Oppède-Le-Vieux.

This was how French novelist Henri Bosco evoked the Luberon, the enchanting land where he had chosen to live. And visitors can in fact see the charming country house and grave of the author of *L'Enfant et la rivière*, or "The Child and the River", in Lourmarin.

Worn, perhaps, old, yes, but majestic is also a fitting description of the Luberon massif, which stretches some sixty kilometres from Cavaillon in the west to Manosque in the east, and covers the Vaucluse to the Alpes-de-Haute-Provence *départements*.

Above
A lavender field close to Viens (left). Cavaillon's Roman arch, at the foot of Saint-Jacques hill (right).

Lourmarin coomb separates *Petit Luberon* from *Grand Luberon*, where the highest point, Mourre Nègre, stands at 1,125 metres. The former is made up of rocky cliffs and the latter, more rounded mountains. Two valleys also run alongside the Luberon, the Durance to the south and the Calavon to the north. This magical land is a patchwork of landscapes – lavender fields, forests, vineyards, limestone hills and ochre cliffs – and is also dotted with the traces of human activity, for instance low walls, dry stone *bories* or huts, walled towns and villages perched up in the hills. It can be explored on foot, by bike and even on horseback.

Cavaillon, the garden of Provence

Cavaillon, part of the Luberon Regional Natural Park, has grown up around the foot of Saint-Jacques hill, a rocky mound of Urgonian limestone overlooking the Durance Valley. Life is easy in this peaceful, typically Provençal town that features tree-lined squares, pavement cafés and some interesting architectural treasures.

Your first trip should be to the 18th-century synagogue – a fine example of French Jewish architecture – with its beautiful rabbi's rostrum and *Musée judéo-comtadin*. There is also Saint-Véran Cathedral with its 14th-century cloister and impressive interior. Its chapels, in particular, are decorated with works by the 17th-century French painters Nicolas and Pierre Mignard.

As an agricultural town and the garden of Provence, Cavaillon also delights visitors with its juicy melons, fine oil and delicious olives, straight from the olive trees of Saint-Jacques hill. Those of you who take the time to climb this hill will be rewarded with a magnificent view of the town and, further a field, the Alpilles, the Luberon and Mont Ventoux, the "giant of Provence".

The road that takes you from Cavaillon to the Aigues area passes close to **Mérindol**. In the 16th century, this village was the capital of the Waldensians, who were ruthlessly persecuted. A discreet memorial bears witness to this violent past.

Below
The village overlooks the Durance Valley.

Above
Merindol Memorial, which pays homage to the Waldensians, who were ruthlessly persecuted in the 16th century.

Above
Ansouis is one of France's Most Beautiful Villages. Be sure to visit its ducal castle.

Below
The remains of La Tour D'Aigues castle, which has suffered greatly throughout its history.

Between the Aigues area and *Grand Luberon*

This area stands out for its beautiful landscapes and traditional villages, which provided refuge for many artists, painters and writers.

It is home to **La Tour-d'Aigues** with its castle, built by the Italian Ercole Nigra, and its earthenware museum, and to **Ansouis** with its lavish ducal castle, owned by the Sabran family of Provence since the 13th century. And finally, **Cadenet**, famous for its basketwork in centuries past and home of the *Tambour d'Arcole*, or "Little Drummer Boy", a young soldier decorated by Napoleon.

Vaugines stands close by with its charming church and then there are the small towns of **Lauris** and **Cucuron**, the former perched on a rocky spur and the latter stationed on the mountainside. Lauris is dotted with beautiful houses and fountains, and is home to the *Jardin Conservatoire des Plantes Tinctoriales,* or Dye Plant Preservation Garden. Here, visitors can learn about the incredible colouring powers of certain plant species, for example, bright red madder and purplish blue true indigo.

In *Les Lettres de mon moulin,* or "Letters from my Windmill" Daudet evoked the village of Cucugnan and its Abbot Martin. For some, it is

Above
The delightful village of Cucuron, which, for some, is said to have inspired Daudet's *Lettres de mon Moulin* and the character of the abbot.

Below
Lauris seen from below with its Dye Plant Preservation Garden and beautiful terraced gardens.

Above
Lauris – a village of character – gradually reveals its picturesque houses and fountains in its narrow stone streets.

Below
Cadenet, or the «Little Drummer Boy's village», has a wonderful view of the Durance Valley.

Cucuron that inspired the writer and for others, the village of Cucugnan, located in the *département* of Aude.

It is in Cucuron that, every May, the men of the village pay homage to St. Tulle, who put an end to the plague epidemic in the 17th century. The strapping fellows cut down the largest poplar tree in the area, sheltering a child from the village, and then carry it on their backs to the church for it to be blessed by the priest.

Before leaving *Grand Luberon*, **Lourmarin** deserves your undivided attention. This village with its three bell towers (belfry, temple and church) knows how much it owes to

Robert Laurent-Vibert. This learned manufacturer from Lyon was passionate about the arts and he saved and restored the village's castle after it fell into disrepair following the French Revolution. The old Gothic-style castle and new Renaissance-style castle are linked by a superb spiral staircase and thanks to this generous patron, the building has also become a kind of Provençal *Villa Médicis*. It is home to a foundation that welcomes artists (musicians, painters and writers) and encourages creation.

Finally, Lourmarin was also a writers' village, as both Henri Bosco and Albert Camus lived here. You can visit the country house of the former, and make out – from a distance only, as his daughter Catherine still lives there – the house of the latter, with its green shutters and round terrace. Camus wrote of this "land that was solemn and austere despite its breathtaking beauty" in his texts.

These two illustrious writers now rest in very simple graves in the village cemetery.

Lourmarin coomb and its delightful road will take you to Bonnieux and the gates of *Petit Luberon*. This site is made up of rocky peaks, cliffs and hilltop villages, which are undeniably among the most beautiful in all of Provence.

Above
A lush garden at the entrance to Lourmarin, which, like many of its Luberon neighbours, is one of France's Most Beautiful Villages.

Below
The village boasts many treasures, including its castle whose Gothic and Renaissance parts are linked by a superb spiral staircase.

Above
The sunlit village of Bonnieux, a former residence of the Knights Templar.

Below
Lacoste, just a few kilometres away.

Bonnieux, Lacoste, Ménerbes and Oppède

The ancient oppidum of **Bonnieux** is said to have been the residence of the Knights Templar until the 14th century, and then papal territory before being returned to France in the late 19th century. Its pyramid-like silhouette conceals a charming village that has magnificent gates and stone passageways, and is crowned by the half-Romanesque, half-Gothic High, or Old, Church. Climb the eighty or so steps to admire its beautiful patina and then go up a little further for a wonderful view of the Calavon plain, the *Monts de Vaucluse* mountain range and Mont Ventoux.

Just two kilometres away, there is an impressive cedar forest that was planted in the 1860s, some 700 metres above sea level. This particular variety of cedar tree comes from the Algerian Middle Atlas and seems very at home here. The enchanting cedar grove, which provides refreshingly cool air, covers 250 hectares over a five-kilometre stretch and follows the range of peaks.

From Bonnieux, the D3 minor road leads you to three more delightful villages.

The first on your route is **Lacoste** with its terraced houses overlooked

by the remains of its castle, which served as a refuge for the 18th-century French libertine writer, the Marquis de Sade. The author of *Philosophy in the Bedroom* lived here for seven years before being imprisoned in the Bastille. It was here, in particular, that he was said to have drawn inspiration for *The 120 days of Sodom*! Following the French Revolution, little remained of the sumptuous residence that the gifted Marquis had decorated in the Renaissance style. Restoration has now begun on the castle but it will take a lot of time... and work.

The site, bought several years ago by French designer Pierre Cardin, is now home to a very prestigious summer festival. Under starry skies, the old stones are now brought to life with the music and speech of opera and plays.

The history of **Ménerbes** is more respectable. This light and peaceful village, resembling a stone ship from a distance, is flanked by two fortresses - the Citadel and the Castellet. The painter Nicolas de Staël and the photographer and painter Dora Maar, who was incidentally Picasso's muse, were both so taken by the village that they chose to call it home. And it was here that Peter Mayle wrote his famous *Year in Provence*, which was later turned into a major Hollywood film.

The hilltop village of **Oppède-le-Vieux**, five kilometres to the west, had a more peculiar fate. This mediaeval fortress was the stronghold of the old Comtat Venaissin area before being expanded in the 16th century and then completely abandoned in favour of the plain. Visitors to the village will no doubt be won over by the indescribable charm of the sleepy old centre, flanked by the recently restored Notre-Dame-d'Alidon Collegiate Church, and the castle ruins.

Above
Quiet Menerbes, which resembles a stone ship from a distance, and its two fortresses.

Below
Thanks to its light and peaceful atmosphere, Menerbes was popular with many artists, including Nicolas de Staël and Dora Maar (left). Oppède is home to the recently restored Notre-Dame d'Alidon Collegiate Church (right).

Apt and the surrounding area, a blend of flavours and colours

French aristocrat and letter writer Marquise de Sévigné described the town as a "huge cauldron of jam" and for good reason, as the town is the capital of candied fruit. The tradition dates back to the late 14th century when fruit, sugar and honey were mixed in huge pans to produce treats for the taste buds. Traditional methods were replaced by industrial production in the late 19th century and an abundance of peach, pear, apple and apricot trees sprang up around Apt. Still today, some 14,000 tons of this local speciality delight food lovers from all corners of the globe.

Apt, Luberon's fortified town, is also a crossroads. It is home to the *Maison du Parc*, Luberon Regional Natural Park's visitor centre, and is set on the route between the Vaucluse plateau and the Alpes-de-Haute-Provence *département*. It is also the starting point for *La Route*

Left

Apt, the capital of candied fruit, is perfect for a stroll with its delightful streets. Here *Rue des Marchands* (above) and the cathedral crypt (below).

Right page

It is impossible not to fall under the charm of Roussillon, which Jean Vilar called "Delphi the Red". Its palette of reds, ochres and yellows is simply magical.

des Ocres, or Ochre Route, that will lure you away from the delicious flavours for a magnificent show of colour.

How can splendid **Roussillon**, that Jean Vilar, founder of the Avignon festival, called *Delphes la rouge*, or "Delphi the Red", ever be put to words? You will instantly be charmed by its maze of narrow streets, its tiny squares, porches and belfry. Carmine reds, bright yellows, pinks... from the walls to the tiled roofs and from the ground to

Above
The Ochre Route, just a short distance from the centre of the village.

Below
Rustrel's Provençal Colorado to the east.

the surrounding steep cliffs, this sunlit village is awash with colour. And the scene is, of course, at its most spectacular at night fall.

Used since Prehistoric times and exploited from the occupation of Provence by the Romans, it was thanks to locally-born Jean-Etienne Astier that ochre became an industrial product. He discovered its properties and unchanging shades in the late 18th century by washing the sand to extract the pigment. Legend has it that the colour of this land was due to a crime of passion but the explanation is more likely to be of geological origin! To the west lies the *Val des Fées*, or Valley of the Fairies. A specially-built path enables visitors to explore the sumptuously-coloured eroded cliffs here, and a little over a kilometre away, the *Conservatoire des ocres* provides a wealth of information on traditional expertise. Those wishing to explore the colour theme further can continue on to Rustrel and its **Provençal Colorado** landscapes to the east.

Gordes, an artists' village carved into the rock face

In their time, the painters Vasarely, Chagall, André Lhote and Pol Mara all had a penchant for Gordes and it is easy to see why! The wonderment is the same whether you discover this stone village, built on a limestone peak of the *Monts de Vaucluse*, from the road or explore its centre. It includes a maze of steep cobbled streets, tall houses built into the rock and an impressive 11th-century castle that was altered during the Renaissance period and restored by Hungarian-born artist Vasarely. The castle is encircled by round towers topped with machicolations – once an effective means of defence – and its walls feature three levels of Renaissance-style windows. These curtain walls also conceal a beautiful spiral staircase and listed fireplace.

Your visit to Gordes would not be complete without a trip to *Le Village des Bories*, made up of dry stone huts with bread ovens and wine vats. Built from the 14th century onwards, these dwellings were abandoned before being restored in the 1950s and 1960s.

Below
The delightful village of Gordes, with its steep cobbled streets and houses built into the rock, enjoys an outstanding natural setting.

Right
The *Village des Bories*. These dry stone huts were built in the 14th century and then abandoned before fortunately being restored.

Above
Sénanque Abbey, a jewel of religious architectural heritage surrounded by lavender fields.

Below
The Cistercian Abbey was founded in 1148 and features a wide nave with three bays, and pillars without capitals.

Sénanque, the young Cistercian sister

A steep road, just two kilometres to the north of Gordes, leads you safely to Sénanque Abbey. This spectacular sight, surrounded by lavender fields, nestles in the hollow of a valley. Together with the abbeys of Le Thoronet and Silvacane, Sénanque is one of the "Cistercian sisters of Provence" and thus observes Cistercian architecture, i.e. a wide nave with three bays and pillars without capitals. Its cloister features semi-circular barrel

The youngest of the three Cistercian sisters of Provence, it is still home to monks today.

vaulted galleries and, surprisingly, capitals decorated with flowers and leaves.

Founded in 1148 by monks from Mazan Abbey, once located in the Vivarais region of France, the youngest of the three sisters derives its name from its natural setting, i.e. *sana aqua*, or healthy water. Although it had its golden age in 1178, the 16th-century French Wars of Religion took a heavy toll on the abbey. It is, however, still home to Cistercian monks today.

Café belle vue
CAFE RESTAURANT
LE BELLEVUE

The Sorgues area and Monts de Vaucluse

Left
L'Isle-sur-la-Sorgue, known as the Comtat's Venice, was built on piles in marshland in the 12th century.
Below
Fontaine de Vaucluse was, for a long time, called Vaucluse-la-Fontaine. It was from here that the Vaucluse *département* derived its name *Vallis Clausa*, meaning enclosed valley.

Fontaine-de-Vaucluse and its mysterious sinkhole

How did the Sorgue River come to have its source at the bottom of a sinkhole? The mystery of this spring – which harbours a cool, fast-flowing river at the foot of a 230-metre cliff – has never really been explained. But this is not for the want of trying, as many dives have been made and the last one, dating from 1989, recorded a depth of 308 metres.

Above
No-one has ever really been able to explain the mystery of the Fontaine sinkhole. How did the Sorgue River come to have its source here?

The sight is no less magical or surprising, however, and the Vaucluse *département* is actually named after this *Vallis Clausa* or Enclosed Valley. In fact, until 1946, Fontaine-de-Vaucluse was called Vaucluse-la-Fontaine.

This village, which has a population of six hundred, also bears a few traces of its many mills (numbering two hundred in the late 19th century). Visitors can even see an old paper embosser in the museum, once the site of a former paper mill.

Between 1337 and 1353, the sheer tranquillity of the village attracted the Florentine poet Petrarch, who proclaimed his love for the beautiful Laura de Noves in his superb collection of poems *Il Canzoniere*, or "The Song Book". A museum library pays tribute to the poet here.

L'Isle-sur-la-Sorgue, the Comtat's Venice

L'Isle-sur-la-Sorgue, which was built on piles in marshland in the 12th century and was an important town in the old Comtat Venaissin area, is today an antique lover's paradise. Some three hundred antique dealers are based here throughout the year and this number more than doubles during the Easter and 15 August holiday weekends.

Its many canals earned it the name of "The Comtat's Venice" but there

Below: Moss-covered paddle wheels in L'Isle-sur-la-Sorgue.

are no gondolas in sight! The town's main boat is in fact the *Nego-chin* (or dog-drowner!), an old flat-bottomed craft that is the star of the traditional July jousting tournaments.

Other unmissable sights in the town are the moss-covered paddle wheels. Once numbering over 60, they were used for corn and fulling mills. The focus of L'Isle is therefore its cool green waters but it also has much to offer in its old centre, including its beautiful Renaissance façades, town houses, alleys and porches. Also do not miss the majestic Collegiate Church of Notre-Dame-des-Anges, rebuilt in the 17th century in the Baroque style.

French poet René Char was born here and in his writing he frequently sang the praises of his town and river "where lightning ends and my house begins». He has, in turn, been honoured by the town through the *Maison René Char*, a museum featuring permanent exhibitions about him and also temporary exhibitions. A few kilometres away, close to the small town of Le Thor, visitors can explore the Thouzon caves, discovered in 1902.

Saumane, the Marquis de Sade's childhood home

This hilltop village takes its name from the French *sommet de l'âne*, or donkey peak. Its small valleys have been turned into dry-stone terraces covered in olive trees, and its small streets are dotted with typical houses and pretty fountains. The castle overlooking the town once belonged to the Marquis de Sade's family. The gifted writer lived here between the ages of five and ten... in the care of his uncle the abbot!

Above

L'Isle abounds in traditional festivals and fairs. It is home to a floating market, held on the local *nego chin* (flat-bottomed boats that can be very unstable for novices!) (left), and antiques fairs, which attract thousands of antique lovers from all over the world each year (right).

Below

The *Château de Thouzon*. This castle, located in the small town of Le Thor, is in fact a former Benedictine monastery. It sits atop a hill on the Comtat Venaissin plain.

12

The old Comtat Venaissin, a land of song, joy and glory

Left page
The town of Carpentras – capital of the Comtat Venaissin – enjoys an exceptional location and features delightful squares and streets, for instance *Rue Calade*.

Carpentras, capital of the Comtat

French writer Frédéric Mistral, a child of the Alpilles, used to sing the praises of this "wet, windy and sunny land, predestined for song, joy and glory".

Once fortified – the 30-metre-high *Porte d'Orange*, or Orange gate, is all that remains of the old ramparts built in the late 14th century –, Carpentras is the capital of the old Comtat Venaissin area. It enjoys an exceptional location, irrigated by the Auzon River and Carpentras Canal, and surrounded by fertile plains, impressive mountains and, slightly further a field, fields of lavender. It makes an ideal base for exploring the neighbouring areas of indescribable natural beauty, for instance Mont Ventoux, the Sault area and the Dentelles de Montmirail mountain range.

Opposite
The prisoners on the Roman arch – all that remains of the Roman era. The arch dates from the 1st century AD and commemorates the Roman victory over the Barbarians.

Above
The beautiful arcades of La Charité cultural centre (left) and Saint-Siffrein Cathedral, built in 1405 (right).

Right
Berlingots, the town's brightly coloured triangular fruit sweets.

But before you set off, spend time exploring the town itself with its charming close-knit streets, squares and 17th- and 18th-century town houses.

In fact, the entire old centre bears the traces of a glorious past. In the 5th century, the town was the seat of a bishopric attached to Arles, and in the early 14th century, it was the residence of the papal legates, who governed the Comtat before it became part of the Vaucluse *département* in 1793.

Carpentras also housed the Jews driven out of the Kingdom of France by Philip IV. Its synagogue, built in the 15th century, stands as a reminder of this period. Still in use today, it is, together with that of Cavaillon, the oldest Jewish place of worship in the Comtat and visi-

tors can admire its beautiful furniture and liturgical objects.

The town can be explored on foot and there are treasures around every corner. Do not cross *Place Aristide-Briand* without stopping off at the *Hôtel-Dieu*, the former hospice. The highlight of the visit is the 18th-century apothecary's shop and its incredible collection of glass phials, jugs and decorated display jars. Monseigneur d'Inguimbert, the altruistic bishop of the town who is buried in the building's chapel, was behind its construction. He was also responsible for the Inguimbertine Library, which holds 220,000 books and boasts the Nicolas-Claude Fabri de Peiresc collection, in honour of the intellectual, astronomer, astrologer and numismatist from Aix.

The bells of Saint-Siffrein Cathedral can be heard from far a field but they are not the only attraction of this building dating from 1405. Its 17th-century sculpted gilded wood Baroque chancel, 15th-century stained glass window panels, and triptych of the *Coronation of the Virgin Mary* by Enguerrand Quarton also deserve your special attention. Finally, there are also the nearby Comtadin and Duplessis Museums, featuring regional objects and art collections, and the Sobirats Museum, a beautiful 18th-century town house with Aubusson tapestries, earthenware, paintings and Empire-style furniture.

A tour of the town would not be complete without mentioning its *berlingots*, the brightly coloured triangular fruit sweets, decorated with a thin white strip of sugar. They come in red, green and yellow, and aniseed, strawberry and lemon flavour. Try them at your leisure as they are very much part of Carpentras!

Above
The *Hôtel Dieu*, or former hospice, which boasts an 18th-century apothecary's shop with an incredible collection of phials and jars.

The Comtat plain and its villages

Pernes-les-Fontaines, seven kilometres to the south, was originally capital of the old Comtat area until Carpentras robbed the small town of its title in 1320. Following a period of prosperity, Pernes-les-Fontaines gradually went into decline before being revived again in the 19th century thanks to an innovative irrigation system.

Set in the heart of a fertile plain, Pernes was named after its 40 or so fountains in 1936. In addition to their delightful gurgling, they bring a welcome coolness to the historic centre with its walls – three of the four original gates can still be seen today –, its old huddled houses, small squares, steep streets, beautiful town houses and chapels. The town also boasts Ferrande Tower, which conceals some remarkably preserved 13th-century frescoes recounting the battles of Charles of Anjou in Italy, and the *Musée du Costume comtadin*, set in a former draper's shop and displaying embroidery, shawls and wedding dresses.

Not far away, stands timeless **Venasque**, the namesake of the old Comtat Venaissin area. This wonderfully preserved, picturesque village is perched in the hills some 300

Left

Pernes is named after its 40 or so fountains that bring a welcome coolness in the height of summer (above). Ferrande Tower conceals some remarkably well preserved 13th-century frescoes (below).

Above

Notre Dame gate, one of the remaining three of the original four gates (left).
Notre-Dame Church in Venasque, a hilltop village 300 metres above sea level (right).

metres above sea level. It is encircled by ramparts and three "Saracen" towers and its very name, *Vindasca*, indicates that it is a white rock that can be seen from a far. Venasque is one of the *département's* seven "most beautiful villages of France" but the majority of its peers are in the Luberon. The jewel of this village, which has a population of 900, is its 6th-century baptistery that has a Greek cross floor plan and was once linked to the former cathedral by a semi-circular vaulted passage. The village's Notre-Dame Church is also well worth a visit.

Head a few kilometres north and you will arrive in **Mazan**. Here, the former Chapel of the White Penitents is home to a *Musée d'Arts et Traditions Populaires*, or Traditional Folk Art Museum, featuring costumes, local archaeological finds and a mineralogical collection (the site is known for its gypsum quarries). The Marquis de Sade also owned a castle here that was the setting for his theatre festival. Unlike Lacoste castle, this building was maintained and is now a sumptuous hotel.

Your tour of the charming villages of the Comtat ends in **Mormoiron**. This delightful mediaeval site, opposite Mont Ventoux, is home to a fascinating *Musée de Musique Mécanique*, or Mechanical Music Museum with old-fashioned charm. Founded by enthusiastic organ builders, this museum provides visitors with an insight into serinettes (early organs), honky tonk pianos, street organs and pianolas.

Mont Ventoux and the Sault area

Left page
Entrechaux.

Below
Mont Ventoux, the "giant of Provence", reaches 1,900 metres at its highest point. It is popular with cyclists and has long been a stage in the Tour de France!

The giant of Provence with its superb views

Mont Ventoux, which reaches 1,909 metres at its highest point, well deserves its nickname of "the giant of Provence"! This magnificent mountain, which keeps watch over the old Comtat Venaissin and the Sault area, can be explored any time of the day or night and in any season. It is also renowned for its lunar-like summit.

If, like Petrarch in 1316, you take the trouble to hike to the top, your arrival at the summit at sunrise will be more than worth the three-hour trek. But the summit is also breathtaking during the day, as when the

Above
Malaucène is the main gate to Mont Ventoux on the north side.

sky is perfectly clear, you can make out Mont Blanc, Canigou mountain, the Dauphiné and Cévennes ranges and sometimes even the Mediterranean Sea beyond Marseille. From Mistral to Aubanel and Giono, stunned poets have time and time again sung the praises of this panoramic view, one of the most far reaching in Europe.

Botanists and nature lovers will also be struck by the highly diverse plant life here. A thousand different plant species are divided into five different levels of vegetation, from 400 to 1,900 metres in altitude. There are Mediterranean plants at the foot of the mountain, then, a little higher up, oak, beech, cedar and Scots pine trees. Mont Ventoux is also dotted with wild flowers, including purple saxifrage, Martagon lilies, houseleeks, lady orchids and sea holly.

As regards wildlife, over 120 bird species, wild boars, mouflon sheep and red deer live together in harmony, and the site is listed as a UNESCO Biosphere Reserve.

Mont Ventoux lends itself to all modes of transport. Walking, of course, but also cycling, as cyclists are fond of – and also dread – the giant of Provence, which has been a stage in the Tour de France since 1951. Racing drivers have also enjoyed competing in hill climbs here for over a century. And when winter comes, you can equip yourself with

Above
On the south side, Bedoin nestles at the foot of the Mont.

skis or a toboggan and slide down its snow-covered slopes. Though unpredictable, the snow that falls here has nevertheless given rise to a small ski resort with some 12 kilometres of slopes. It has to be said that this is somewhat unique for Provence!

On either side of Mont Ventoux, there are many charming stone villages and large market towns that are worth the detour.

Take, for example, **Malaucène** with its tree-lined river, its old centre dotted with narrow streets and fountains, and Saint-Michel's Church whose Romanesque bell tower and west façade contrast its Gothic chancel and chapels. It is the main gate to Mont Ventoux on the north side.

Rather than forming a single village, **Beaumont-du-Ventoux** is made up of nine picturesque hamlets, scattered along the minor road and often featuring pretty chapels.

On the south side, **Bédoin**, nestling at the foot of the Mont, prides itself on having the largest municipal forest in France (6,100 hectares in all). It is a major stopover village for cyclists heading towards Mont Ventoux, and it also features a beautiful parish church with an altarpiece by French painter Nicolas Mignard.

Above
Sainte-Madeleine *croque-moines*, or crunchy almond biscuits. You'll find this speciality, made by the monks, in the abbey shop.

Below
The pretty mediaeval village of Le Barroux, which has grown up around its keep.

Right page
Sainte-Madeleine Abbey attracts many traditionalists for its Sunday morning Mass.

The mediaeval village of **Le Barroux**, set between the Comtat Venaissin and Malaucène plains, is stationed on a rocky peak. It has grown up around its keep, and its fortified castle was the seat of the feudal lords from the 12th to the 15th centuries. Part of this castle now belongs to the Vayson de Pradenne family and is under restoration, while its chapel and terrace belong to the village and can be visited in their current state. Other sights in the village include Sainte-Madeleine Abbey. Many traditionalists flock here every Sunday morning for its Gregorian Mass.

Above
Sault derives its name from *saltus*, or wooded area interspersed with clearings. Sault is lavender country.

Below
In Aurel too the blue carpets of lavender stretch for as far as the eye can see.

The Sault area, filled with flavours and colours

With its blue carpets of lavender stretching as far as the eye can see, its fields of golden spelt and its dense forests – Sault in fact derives its name from *saltus*, or wooded area interspersed with clearings –, the Sault area promises visitors a wide variety of colours and never-ending, wild landscapes. Flavours are also important here and thanks to its lavender honey, spelt, suckling lambs, nougat and macaroons, it is a leading destination for food lovers.

Sault-en-Provence, the former capital of the county, is also stationed on a rocky spur and makes an ideal base for exploring the neighbouring Nesque gorge and Le Toulourenc valley.

Very little remains of its feudal castle and ramparts but the old town is made up of mediaeval houses, Renaissance residences and interesting town houses. Notre-Dame-de-la-Tour Church also blend genres and periods with its Romanesque nave and pointed bar-

rel vault, its altered sanctuary and its 19th-century northern side aisle. Just two kilometres from the village, the *Jardin des Lavandes*, or Lavender Farm, also delights visitors with its two hundred varieties of the *Lavandula* genus.

From Sault, you have the choice between heading north to Le Toulourenc Valley or south towards the Nesque gorge.

Aurel, 5 kilometres to the north, stands opposite the Baronnies hills. This mediaeval stone village enjoys wonderful light and, like many of its neighbours, is popular with designers, potters and painters. French artist Pierre Ambrogiani, in particular, stayed here for 11 years between 1950 and 1961 and paved the way for others.

If you head even further north, you will reach **Montbrun-les-Bains**, which also prides itself on being one of the "most beautiful villages

Above
The lavender fields are regularly tended to and celebrated with a large festival every August.
Below
The village of Montbrun-les-Bains.

Above
Brantes, close to Mont Ventoux, is a real eyrie with zigzagging streets that overlooks Toulourenc River.

of France". Set in the heart of the Provencal Drôme, this pretty mediaeval spa town is blessed with a rich heritage and if you wander up and down its steep, narrow streets you will come across its church, belfry and castle.

From here, a winding minor road takes you to **Brantes**, ten or so kilometres away. This village, a real eyrie with zigzagging streets, overlooks the Toulourenc River. As you explore it in the shadow of the impressive Mont Ventoux, you will stumble upon earthenware makers, a figurine maker and the ruins of a feudal castle that was undoubtedly magnificent in its time.

Press on and you will arrive in peaceful **Saint-Léger-du-Ventoux**, the smallest village of the *département* with only 24 inhabitants. You will then be near the **Toulourenc River** (meaning "all or nothing"), the largest river fed by Mont Ventoux, after the Fontaine-de-Vaucluse spring. It runs for 30 kilometres, from Aulan Castle to the Ouvèze Valley.

On the other side of Sault, to the east, you will come across the **Albion plateau**, which probably derives its name, *alba*, from the light colour of the rock and vegetation. This splendid and austere site was often chosen as a backdrop by novelist Jean Giono, a child of the area. The heart of the plateau is studded with villages and several interesting churches, for example, the listed Romanesque Trinity Church in Saint-Trinit and Saint-Christol Church.

To the west of Sault, you will be taken aback by the incredible contrast offered by **Nesque Gorge**, a spectacularly deep and mysterious valley surrounded by unbelievably flat plateaus!

The Romanesque Chapel of Saint-Michel d'Anesca (or Saint-Michel de la Nesque) nestles at the very bottom of the gorge, on the edge of the stream. It dates from the 12th century and was restored in the 17th century. The gorge is also home to the *Rocher-du-Cire*, or Wax Rock, which conceals wild bee hives, and

the Castellaras viewpoint, specially designed for a monument dedicated to Frédéric Mistral.

When reaching this panoramic viewpoint, you will easily understand the words written by the poet after he discovered the site in 1866: "The Nesque plunges into a dark rocky gorge and there comes a point when the rock suddenly, and surprisingly, rears up to form the Wax Rock. I can assure you that no cat, goat or satyr will ever climb it!"

Above
Less famous than its Ardèche neighbour, the Nesque gorge is nevertheless worth the detour for its spectacularly deep and mysterious valley.

Below
The village of Saint Trinit, set in the heart of the area and the Albion plateau, stands 859 metres above sea level and features a delightful 12th-century listed church. Every second Sunday in October, it hosts a mushroom festival.

Around the *Dentelles de Montmirail* mountain range, breathtaking landscapes and tiny villages

Left page and below
The *Dentelles de Montmirail* hills with their finely sculpted limestone peaks. Their silvery-grey cliffs are a favourite with climbers from all four corners of the globe.

These hills with finely sculpted limestone peaks and steep, jagged cliffs really are a sight to behold! The **Dentelles de Montmirail**, or Montmirail Laces, do not owe their pointed shape to the talented, steady hand of a lace maker, as their name suggests, but rather to natural erosion. These beautiful silvery-grey cliffs, whose summit, Saint-Amand peak, stands at 734 metres, are a favourite with climbers. They also provide a dream setting for hikers and are surrounded by lush and varied countryside studded with tiny villages and vines.

Above
The Montmirail area is also dotted with towns and villages. Gigondas and Vacqueyras, in particular, are known for their delicious wines, which are exported throughout the world.

Nearby Beaumes-de-Venise, Vacqueyras and Gigondas have all given their names to heavenly nectars. The former is renowned for its syrupy Muscat sweet wine, and the latter two for their powerful, solidly structured red wines. Then, while on your way to Vaison-la-Romaine, do not forget to stop off in Sablet and then Séguret, home to a living nativity scene on Christmas Eve.

The name Beaumes comes from *baumes* – caves dug into the sandstone and troglodyte dwellings – while Venise refers to the old Comtat Venaissin area where

Left page, below
The village of Gigondas, known as *Jocunditas* by the Romans.

Above
The peaceful village of Sablet, which comes alive during its July book festival.

Below
Beaumes-de-Venise has won fame for its sweet Muscat wine. In the background, Notre-Dame d'Aubunes Chapel.

Beaumes-de-Venise nestles at the foot of a hill.

In this village, which is sheltered from the mistral wind, you can visit Saint-Hilaire Chapel, and Notre-Dame d'Aubune Chapel whose 12th-century bell tower is a listed monument.

Four kilometres northeast, the narrow streets of **Vacqueyras** converge towards a church featuring a Provençal bell tower and a 12th-century watchtower. This village is the main gateway to the Dentelles mountain range.

Not far from there, **Gigondas**, once part of the Principality of Orange, was named *Jocunditas* – meaning joy and elation – by the Romans. There is a real sense of calm emanating from this village and if you take a couple of sips of wine in the scorching sun you will begin to feel some of the joy and elation that its first inhabitants experienced! A steep path will lead you up to the 17th-century hospice buildings where you can enjoy a wonderful panoramic view. These buildings are now home to an open-air theatre, and leading opera singers capture the hearts of audiences here in the summer months.

By contrast, the small, peaceful

Above
The village of Seguret

Above
Just like Rome, Vaison-la-Romaine is surrounded by seven hills. It was in turn Celtic, Roman and, at one stage, even part of Gascony! Here, the upper town.

town of **Sablet** is much favoured by writers, especially during the *Journées du livre*, or Book Days, in July.

Séguret, the hub of Provençal traditions, resembles a nativity scene... and for good reason, as on every Christmas Eve since 1960 its inhabitants have celebrated the *Mystère des bergers*, or Mystery of the Shepherds. Village people of all ages relive the night before Christmas in the quaint little church of Saint-Denis, and visitors come from far afield to witness the scene.

Nestling at the foot of a hill, the village is overlooked by the tower of a former medieval castle. Visitors can enjoy wandering up and down its steep, cobbled streets to discover its old houses, fountains and wash-houses, and from the church square there is a breathtaking view that has earned Séguret the name "Balcony of the Haut-Comtat".

At the crossroads of the Baronnies hills, Dentelles de Montmirail mountains and Comtat plain, still heading north, you will reach **Vaison-la-Romaine**, a town surrounded by seven hills... just like Rome.

Marked by an eventful history, the town was in turn Celtic, Roman, Episcopal and even, at one stage, part of Gascony! It began life as the capital of the *Vocontii*, a Celtic tribe, and in 125 B.C., *Veisoun*, as it is called in Provençal, welcomed the Romans. It then enjoyed relative independence in the heart of a land divided into four areas. After the fall of the Roman Empire, Vaison – the seat of a powerful bishopric – reigned over forty villages and this was enough to capture the interest of the Counts of Toulouse, who chose to build a new town and castle on the rock.

Today, Vaison is divided into two parts – the old, upper town and new, lower town – but both are of equal standing.

The upper, mediaeval town is a stone showcase with narrow streets paved with pebbles from the Ouvèze Valley. From the ruins of its castle, reached by crossing a 20-metre-long Roman bridge that straddles the Ouvèze River and

Below left
The 20-metre-long Roman bridge that straddles the Ouvèze River

passing underneath a fortified gate, there is an unrestricted view of the town and Mont Ventoux.

By comparison, the lower town is the very heart of Vaison with its market and shops. But it also features some beautiful archaeological remains, including the *Villa des Messii* – the foundations of a Roman villa –, the Puymin and La Villasse sites, and the ancient theatre. Though more modest than its neighbour in Orange, this theatre nevertheless deserves a visit. And if you find yourself in Vaison during *Les Choralies* – a choir singing festival held in August every three years –, you will be overwhelmed by the magical voices and sweet music that fill the air. Choir singers occupy every available square, church or school to perform gospel and jazz variations and even Gregorian chant.

Below right
The town features some beautiful archaeological remains, including the ancient theatre and La Villasse site.

The Rhône Valley

Left page and below
Châteauneuf-du-Pape is famous throughout the world for its wine. Its stony, quartz and sandy clay soil is ideal for the vines.

Châteauneuf-du-Pape, wonderful vineyards for wonderful wine!

The history of Châteauneuf began in 1094 when its former name, *Castro novo*, was mentioned for the first time in an official document. Popes Clement V and Clement VII regularly stayed here but it was John XXII who inextricably linked the history of the village to that of the papacy by having a castle built here in the 14th century. The castle suffered heavily during World War II

Below
The *Château des Fines Roches*, set just a few kilometres away from Châteauneuf-du-Pape, used to belong to the Marquis Folco de Baroncelli and is today a luxury hotel.

but a beautiful room with a vaulted ceiling still remains today.

History aside, Châteauneuf-du-Pape is above all a vineyard that is famous throughout the world. The vines here enjoy ideal natural conditions, such as stony soil (mainly composed of rolled quartz and sandy red clay), a dry and sunny climate, and of course the prevailing mistral wind.

The Bishop of Avignon owned vines in Châteauneuf as early as 1157, and there were reportedly 300 hectares in the 13th century. Today, the Castel-Papal vineyard features 13 *cépages*, or types of vine, and covers no fewer than 3,000 hectares and includes Châteauneauf and land from four neighbouring towns (Sorgues, Courthézon, Bédarrides and Orange). It was the literary *Félibres*, led by Frédéric Mistral and Anselme Mathieu, who happily sampled this wine, which brought "courage, song, love and joy"!

From here, you can travel 10 kilometres along a peaceful minor road to the town of Orange…

Above and below: A treasure among treasures, Orange's ancient theatre is one of the best preserved of the Roman era. Some of the most prestigious opera singers perform at the foot of this wall during the *Les Chorégies* opera festival, held every summer. Verdi and Rossini, in particular, benefit from the theatre's excellent acoustics.

Orange, from the Romans to the Dutch...

For those of you who still doubt that Orange, set at the foot of Saint-Eutrope hill, was a glorious Roman capital, then the sight of its two treasures – the ancient theatre and triumphal arch – should be more than enough to convince you.

The prestigious theatre is one of the best preserved from the Roman era alongside the one in Aspendos, Turkey. Did Louis XIV not refer to its stage wall as "the most beautiful wall of our entire kingdom"? A statue of Augustus can be seen in a niche at the foot of the wall and the theatre's outer wall, measuring 100 metres in length and 37 in height, has doors leading to the dressing rooms. The site was restored in the early 19th century and thanks to its excellent acoustics, it has hosted *Les Chorégies* – once of France's most prestigious opera festivals – since 1869. Its very name, from the Greek word *choreos*, takes us back to the Greco-Roman period and some of the most amazing voices perform Verdi, Puccini, Rossini and Bizet here each summer.

Above
Like the ancient theatre, the Roman arch is one of the town's treasures. It was built in the 1st century to celebrate the achievements of the 2nd Gallic Legion.

Right page, top
A Barry troglodyte dwelling (left). The Rasteau vineyard, famous for its sweet natural wine (right).

Right page, bottom
Mornas fortress stands on a 137-metre-high cliff and protects the sleepy village below. It has a wonderful view of Mont Ventoux, the *Dentelles de Montmirail* range and the Rhône Valley.

The town's other Roman treasure, the triumphal arch, built in the 1st century to celebrate the achievements of the 2nd Gallic Legion, is located at the northern entrance to the town.

At the end of the 12th century, Bertrand des Baux took the title of Prince of Orange and transformed the town into a principality, enclosed within the Comtat soil. It then fell into the hands of the Dutch royal family, the Orange-Nassau, in the 16th century. The Treaty of Utrecht sealed the return of Orange to France in 1713, but the Dutch royal family has since retained the name of Orange and the colour is paraded during national holidays and even football matches!

Finally, Notre-Dame-de-Nazareth Cathedral, whose portal is typical of Romanesque Provençal architecture, and the museum, which features paintings and archaeological collections, round off this list of Orange's treasures.

The *Nationale 7* holiday road!

To the north of Orange, on the way up to the Enclave des Papes on the *Nationale 7*, you can stop off in some lovely little villages. There is **Piolenc**, home to a delightful museum that is devoted to the said main road, which was brought to fame by French singer Charles Trenet's song, *Route National 7*. Next comes **Sérignan-du-Comtat**, where the French botanist and entomologist Jean-Henri Fabre set up his home and office, *l'Harmas*. It still features his herbariums, collections of insects and fossils, and 20,000 plates. And finally, there are the charming villages of **Sainte-Cécile-les-Vignes**, **Rasteau** and **Cairanne** which are worth the detour for their fine wines (that is if Châteauneuf has not already quenched your thirst)!

These villages can be reached by the D975 and D976 minor roads.

A trip to the north of the Vaucluse département:

Enclave des Papes, Provençal Drôme and the Baronnies hills

Left
Set in the heart of Provençal Drôme, La Garde-Adhémar has retained its ramparts and overlooks Pierrelatte Plain. Here, the Jardin des Herbes botanical garden.

Below
Notre-Dame-de Nazareth Church in Valréas. Do not miss its beautiful listed organ.

Enclave des Papes, a corner of Vaucluse in the Drôme *département*

To the north of Vaucluse and Provence, there is an unusual historic and territorial feature, L'Enclave des Papes, or the Popes' Enclave. This name was retained by the *canton*, or district, of Valréas, which is today made up of the 9,500-strong town of Valréas and three other, neighbouring villages. L'Enclave des Papes is, in fact, a part of the Vaucluse *département* nestling in the Drôme *département*, and to better understand this oddity you will have to go back to the 14th century.

In the beginning, the town of Valréas belonged to several feudal lords. Then, in 1317, it came under the authority of the States of the Holy See, as the popes bought it from the Dauphin of France along with Visan, Richerenches and then Grillon. It remained papal territory for four centuries until it was returned to Vaucluse during the French Revolution.

Today, the charming town of **Valréas**, which has gradually grown up around its fortified castle, bears the traces of its religious history in its buildings. It boasts the Romanesque Church of Notre-Dame-de-Nazareth,

Above
Visan harmoniously blends beautiful town houses with the vestiges of its Dauphin ramparts.

with its listed gilded and polychromic wood organ; two chapels (*Chapelle des Pénitents blancs* with its rich decor and beautiful cast iron portal, and the *Chapelle des Pénitents noirs*), and two convents – of the Ursulines and Conventual Franciscans. The latter features a tower, decorated with four sundials, that was one of the first examples of Italian Renaissance-style architecture in France. Finally, the town even has a Protestant church.

You can also visit the *Château de Simiane*, a splendid building that dates back to mediaeval times and now holds the town hall. A tour of the building reveals beautiful rooms with French-style ceilings and sculpted walls, and in summer, the *Salon de l'Enclave* is the setting for an exhibition on Provençal painters. Finally, the *Musée du Cartonnage et de l'Imprimerie*, or Cardboard and Printing museum, will take you back

Below
Grillon boasts the beautifully renovated *Maison du Boulanger, Maison des Trois Arcs* and *Maison Milon*, today home to a research centre (left). The library in *Château de Simiane* (right).

to the 19th century, when Valréas was the European capital of the cardboard industry. It was, in fact, Frenchman Ferdinand Revoul who invented the cardboard box in 1840.

And do not overlook the area around Valréas and the other three villages in the Enclave either.

Grillon, to the west, features a mediaeval part protected by 13th-century ramparts and **Visan**, to the south, has retained the ruins of its mediaeval castle and a few vestiges of the Dauphin and Pope ramparts. Its narrows streets are lined with beautiful town houses.

Finally, **Richerenches** also has a few treats in store for visitors. The old village with its fortress-like feel is home to one of the best preserved Knights Templar residences in France. The truffle also takes prides of place here, so if you are passing through Richerenches in January, do not miss the Truffle Mass, a delightful and unusual ceremony that raises funds to restore the small parish church.

Above
Richerenches is also reputed for its delicious truffles, celebrated with a delightful Mass every January.

Below
Richerenches is worth the detour as it is home to one of the best preserved Knights Templar residences in France.

Above
Notre-Dame d'Aiguebelle Trappist Abbey. The shop features a wide range of essential-oil based products and a large music and book section. There are religious works, of course, but also history and tourist books (left). *Château de Suze-la-Rousse* (right).

Below
Grignan was long popular with the Marquise de Sévigné, who stayed with her son-in-law here and today lies in the collegiate church.

Grignan, in the footsteps of the Marquise de Sévigné…

Head a little further north and you will arrive in the heart of Provençal Drôme, where numerous hilltop or fortified villages, criss-crossed with narrow paved streets or covered passageways, are dotted throughout the outstanding countryside. They overlook valleys and yet are concealed by endless carpets of lavender fields and vineyards.

Saint-Paul-Trois-Châteaux, in the natural and historic Tricastin region, boasts a magnificent cathedral, beautiful town houses and a Tricastin archaeological museum. Many of its buildings feature light-coloured local limestone, found in abundance in neighbouring quarries. A few kilometres to the north, **La Garde-Adhémar**, perched on a headland overlooking Pierrelatte plain and Donzère canal, is one of the "most beautiful villages of France". Its winding streets, lined with old houses, are today home to numerous artists and craftspeople.

Magnificent **Grignan** is largely dedicated to the French letter writer Madame de Sévigné, who stayed here from 1694 to 1696, the year of her death. She now lies in the 16th-century collegiate church, whose flat roof serves as a terrace. Grignan is today brought to life by a letter writing festival and delightful evening events, held in the summer months in honour of this famous writer. The Renaissance castle – residence of the Count of Grignan, son-in-law to Madame de Sévigné – also partly owes its fame to the Marquise. To reach the castle, climb the narrow snaking streets from the old village. When you arrive at the foot of the building, which was destroyed during the French Revolution, restored during the 20th century and has since been fully refurnished, be sure to cast your eyes over its superb façade and explore the Gothic gallery. As for the south terrace, it offers a breathtaking view of the Comtat plain, Mont Ventoux and the *Dentelles de Montmirail* mountain range.

Above
13th- and 15th-century murals in Saint-Paul-Trois-Châteaux Cathedral.

Below
It is not strictly Provence and not quite the old Dauphiné province... but Provençal Drôme, an unrivalled enclave, and the Dieulefit area.

Right The mediaeval village of Mollans-sur-Ouvèze, roughly 10 kilometres from Vaison. It features the delightful stone Dauphins' fountain and pretty washhouse with six arcades.

Below The Randonne Tower, built c. 1280 by the Baroness de Montauban, is the emblem of the town. It served as both a keep and military prison for the castle.

The Baronnies hills, a fruitful land

The Baronnies hills, located even further north but a little to the east this time, are made up of eroded limestone plateaus, hemmed in by the Eygues Valley to the north and Mont Ventoux to the south. They form a patchwork of colours and crops, as the local climate of fre-

quent sunshine, moderate wind and varied soils is perfect for lavender, olive trees (no fewer than 250,000 of them can be found in the AOC quality label area), and lime trees. In fact, the area is responsible for three quarters of French national lime blossom production.

Nyons, set between Mediterranean Provence and the Prealps, is famous for its olives and delicious oil. The olive variety here is called the *tanche* and in June the trees abound in delicate white flowers that later turn to fruit.

Tanche olives are harvested in December and January when slightly wrinkled by the cold. They are then taken to the local mills where they are pickled (for at least six months) or pricked and dry cured. In fact, the town has a museum devoted to olive farming in *Allée des Tilleuls*, or Lime Tree Alley, of all places!

In addition to its gastronomic heritage, Nyons also boasts interesting architectural treasures from its fortified mediaeval town and church with its 14th-century bell tower to its old olive oil mills and Romanesque bridge, which took 70 years to build.

There are also churches and chapels to visit in the neighbouring villages of **Mirabel-aux-Baronnies** and **Piégon**.

Finally, to the southeast of Nyons, the historical centre of **Buis-les-Baronnies** features a quaint and lively market square, a beautiful church and the *Maison des Plantes Aromatiques*, or Aromatic and Medicinal Plant Museum, which is full of information and delicious scents!

Above Every Thursday, Nyons is brought to life by its market. This whirl of colours, flavours and perfumes is also dotted with potters' stands.

Below The Romanesque church of Notre-Dame de Beauvert in Saint-Jalle (left). The village of Buis-les-Baronnies (right).

The Provence of Cézanne and Giono

A stroll through the Aix area in the footsteps of Cézanne...

Left page
Sainte-Victoire mountain, which was a constant source of inspiration for the painter Paul Cézanne, is crisscrossed with hiking trails.
Below
The recently-restored *Cours Mirabeau* boulevard is the heart of Aix, particularly on market day.

Aix, a source of inspiration for painters and writers alike

Aix-en-Provence prides itself on its 300 days of sunshine a year and you can soak up this glorious sun, doze peacefully on a warm pavement café or enjoy the shade of the plane trees or Sainte-Victoire mountain.

The town of Aix was home to French painter Paul Cézanne. He was born here in 1839, died here in 1906 and painted his much-loved mountain – Sainte-Victoire – over 60 times. If you are looking for a good way to explore this rich city, you can follow in the painter's

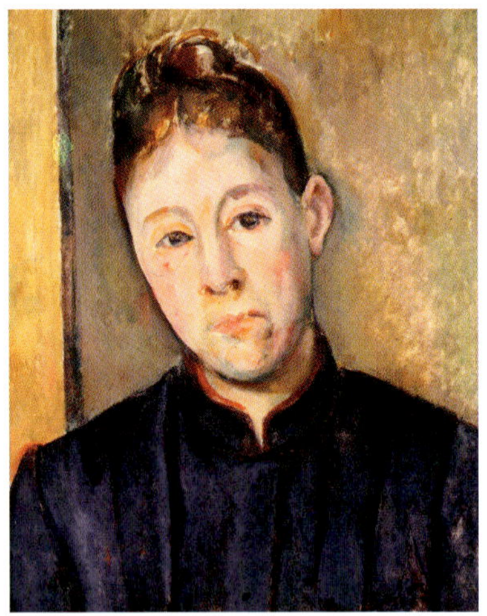

Above *Musée Granet* holds many treasures, including Cézanne's masterpieces *Portrait de Madame Cézanne* (left) and *Les Baigneuses* (right). (Musée Granet Aix-en-Provence, photo Bernard Terlay CPA).

Below Saint-Sauveur Cathedral, one of the gems of Aix's architectural heritage. It was built on the site of an ancient Roman forum and combines various different styles, including a Provençal Romanesque nave and cloister, a Gothic nave, a Merovingian baptistery with a Renaissance dome, and a Baroque nave.

footsteps via a well-designed circuit, available as a leaflet from the tourist information centre. This trail will lead you to the artist's house, his schools, his favourite cafés, his workshop and even the *Atelier des Lauves*, built on the hill of the same name away from the hustle and bustle of the city. This haven of peace was built in such a way that he could tirelessly admire his Sainte-Victoire.

While you are in the area, you should also visit the *Musée Granet*. It was home to the city's art school and it was precisely here that the artist obtained his second drawing prize at the age of 20. Following the prolific *Cézanne en Provence* exhibition in 2006 in honour of the painter, the renovated *Musée Granet* now exhibits all its permanent collections, including eight works by Cézanne – from the *Baiser de la muse* (Muse's Kiss) to *Les Baigneuses* (Bathers) and the *Portrait de Madame Cézanne* (Portrait of Madame Cézanne).

The more modern Vasarely foundation, just 3 kilometres from the city centre, is also well worth the trip. In addition to temporary exhibitions, it features 42 of the artist's life size works, designed to favour the integration of art into architecture.

Aix therefore fires the imagination and has inspired artists and writers alike. It prides itself on having raised French writer Emile Zola during his early years and it was here that Zola met Cézanne and their 30-year friendship began. The author in fact paid reference to Aix in five of his set of 20 novels, collectively known as *Les Rougon-Macquart*. Aix became Flassans, Mirabeau River was renamed the Sauvaire and Sainte-Victoire became the Garrigues… but it is unmistakably the Aix area that Zola chose as the backdrop for this family saga.

In 122 B.C., the creation of *Aquae Sextiae* (or Waters of Sextius, after the consul who, with his army, besieged the Salyes people of the Entremont oppidum) marked the first Roman settlement in Gaul. In 1182, the city – which was now home to the Counts of Provence – grew up around the count's palace, Saint-Sauveur Cathedral and the craftsmen's district.

In 1471, Aix become a royal city when good King René settled here and, after the return of Provence to France, it was the site of the new *parlement*, or law courts, and the centre of Provençal government from 1501 onwards. The following century witnessed considerable urban development. The Villeverte and Mazarin districts were built, closely followed by *Place d'Albertas* and the *Hôtel-de-Ville*, or town hall. The modern-day *Cours Mirabeau* boulevard (then an avenue for coaches built in 1650) was also widened. Aix finally woke from a long slumber in the second half of the 20th century and is today a lively university town and centre for art and culture. Try and coincide your visit with one of its prestigious festivals. Its July opera festival is a particular favourite with music lovers.

Aix has remained a charming city and its warm-coloured stone and tiled roofs offer a pleasing architectural harmony. The heart of the town happily reveals itself to anyone who takes the time to explore its maze of streets. It conceals quaint little squares, a multitude of fountains (40 at the very least, including the Quatre-Dauphins, Espéluque, Rotonde and Albertas ones), interlaced cobbled alleys, sumptuous town houses, and parks and castles

The highlights of its religious heritage and architecture include the *Palais de l'Archevêché*, or Archbishop's Palace, Saint-Sauveur Cathedral and Sainte-Catherine Chapel, which especially stands out for its façade.

Finally, the city is also inextricably linked to the famous *calisson*, a sweet made from marzipan, candied melon or apricots, unleavened bread and sugar. Though its origins are disputed – some think the speciality comes from Italy –, the people of Aix believe that the small, sugary, diamond-shaped sweet dates back to the time of King René. It is said that a courtier in the company of the king's betrothed, who was renowned for her bad temper but on this occasion was charmed by the delightful white sweets, exclaimed, *Di cali soun* ("They are hugs" in Provençal!).

Above There is not a street or square in Aix that does not feature some kind of architectural delight – close up of *Hôtel d'Albertas* (left), Quatre Dauphins' fountain (right).

Below The *Pavillon de Vendôme*, or Vendôme Villa, was built on the orders of the Duke of Vendôme for his passionate love affair with the *Belle du Canet*, Lord of Canet's beautiful widow. The villa's main façade features the three Classical orders and is surrounded by splendid French-style gardens. The interior is decorated with portraits, Provençal furniture and temporary modern art exhibitions.

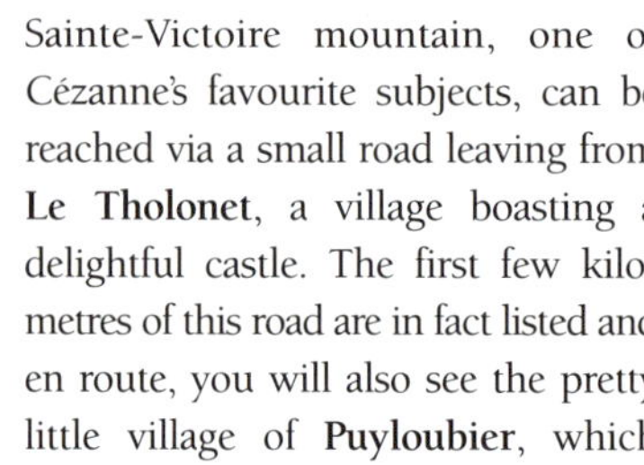

Right
The impressive Gothic basilica that overlooks the mediaeval village of Saint-Maximin.

Below
Do not miss Silvacane Abbey, the first of the Cistercian abbeys in Provence (before Sénanque and Le Thoronet). It is a fine and rare example of pure lines and sobriety.

The Aix area, between Sainte-Baume and Sainte-Victoire

Sainte-Victoire mountain, one of Cézanne's favourite subjects, can be reached via a small road leaving from **Le Tholonet**, a village boasting a delightful castle. The first few kilometres of this road are in fact listed and en route, you will also see the pretty little village of **Puyloubier**, which backs onto the impressive mountain. This village derives its name from *Podium luberium* (meaning wolf mountain) and conceals a beautiful church and several rural chapels.

The 60-kilometre circuit around the mountain has many surprises in store and the views are every bit as magical as in Cézanne's colourful paintings.

Further south, the Sainte-Baume mountain ridge has a truly sacred aura. Stretching over 12 kilometres from west to east, the ridge looms up to the north of Aubagne from the Baou de Bertagne to the Baou de Saint-Cassien. It has an average altitude of close to 1,000 metres above sea level and measures 1,147 metres at its highest point. The small village of **Gémenos** stands at the gates to the ridge whose southern slope features a Mediterranean forest and whose northern slope is dotted with cliffs, beech trees, lime trees and ivy. It is said that Mary Magdalene lived in a cave here for 30 years and in Provençal, *baoumo* means cave in a rock, hence the name of the mountain ridge. This is why the site is so revered by the people of Provence today, and every Easter Monday it is the setting for a seven-hour procession.

While in the area, be sure to pay a visit to **Saint-Maximin**. This medi-

Above
Salon-de-Provence is home to Saint-Laurent Collegiate Church, built c. 1344 (left), and the *Tour de l'Horloge*, or Clock Tower (right).

aeval village, whose old districts are still well defined, is organised around a beautiful basilica. This religious building, one of the most impressive examples of Gothic architecture in Provence, features interesting furniture and works of art, including its famous organs, created by Dominican monk and organ maker Jean-Esprit Isnard and his nephew Joseph Isnard. The village also features a Royal Dominican Convent, built by the Avignon architect Jean-Baptiste Franque between 1750 and 1785.

Those of you wishing to explore the Aix area even further can continue on to **Fuveau**, a picturesque sentinel in the Arc Valley; **Trets**, a charming village that is still encircled by walls, and **Cabriès**, stationed at the top of a rocky peak. Heading further north still, you will come across peaceful **Jouques** to the east and **La Roque-d'Anthéron** to the west. In addition to hosting one of the world's most prestigious piano festivals, the latter is home to the magnificent Silvacane Abbey whose stained glass windows were created by Turkish-born artist Sarkis in 2001.

Salon de Provence

Salon de Provence is home to the *Patrouille de France* – the French Air Force's acrobatic demonstration team – and it also welcomed the famous astronomer Nostradamus, who lived out the last 20 years of his life here from 1547. His former house is, in fact, open to visitors and features a waxworks retracing his life in addition to temporary exhibitions and a library holding precious works.

But Salon de Provence, which enjoys a prime location between the Luberon, Arles, and Avignon, has much more to offer.

Your first stop should be the *Château-musée de l'Emperi*, one of the most impressive mediaeval fortresses in Provence. This former residence of the archbishops of Arles, and then the kings of France, still features a beautiful Renaissance gallery and main courtyard, which hosts a reputed festival every year. Still on the theme of architectural heritage, Saint-Laurent Collegiate Church was built c. 1344, and the *Chapelle de la Vierge* holds Nostradamus' tomb.

Finally, the famous Marseille soap is also made in Salon! The town is, in fact, close to the Alpilles range with its olive oil, and the Camargue region with its sodium and salt, all essential soap-making ingredients. The traditional *Savonnerie Marius Fabre* and *Savonnerie Rampal Patou* soap factories still produce soap today and are open to the public, as is the *Musée du savon de Marseille*, housed in a former drying room. It features a delightful collection of soap moulding machines, stencils and old packaging. Of course it all smells good and you will leave with plenty of natural products!

Haute-Provence, Jean Giono's Imaginary South

Left page
The small village of Montfuron, close to Manosque, and its fully restored windmill.

Below
Lure mountain, which, together with Valensole plateau, formed the harsh yet beautiful backdrop for the works of Jean Giono, who spoke of an "Imaginary South".

It is not quite the Alps and no longer really part of Provence but Haute-Provence is, in fact, both at once.

Multi-faceted and lush, it covers some 7,000 square kilometres. Half of the Alpes-de-Haute-Provence *département* is, in fact, made up of Regional Natural Parks. Charming Provençal villages, the delightful town of Manosque and its hills, the Durance Valley, Lure mountain, Valensole plateau and, further afield, Verdon Gorge, are just some of the star attractions that make up what the Manosque-bred writer referred to as the "Imaginary South". Most of his works were in fact written in this setting.

Above

Behind the thick wall, the peaceful centre of Manosque comes alive on market day (left). Saunerie gate, with its machicolated turrets, dates from 1382. It was named after the *saunerie*, or salt works, that used to be located nearby (right).

Delightful Manosque

Jean Giono – the author of *Colline* and *Jean le Bleu* – loved using his town as a backdrop for his writing. He referred to it as a "tortoise's shell in the grass" and depicted it wonderfully in his novels. In *Le Hussard sur le toit*, or "The Hussar on the Roof", for example, his hero Angelo found refuge on the town's roofs during a cholera outbreak. Jean Giono long praised Manosque and, in turn, the town now honours its writer. You can therefore see his humble birthplace at No. 14 Rue Grande – formerly a wealthy road and now a shopping street –, and visit the centre that bears his name. The *Centre Jean Giono*, set up in a former town house, recounts the life of the writer through the permanent exhibition *Giono le voyageur immobile*, or "Giono the Immobile Traveller". The centre's library also features his many works in both French and foreign languages.

Following in Giono's wake, Manosque has raised other noteworthy writers – for example Pierre Magnan and René Fregni –, and the town celebrates literature every autumn with its *Correspondances* festival.

Manosque is also worth the detour for the sheer calm found behind its thick, tree-lined wall. This wall conceals a pretty old centre that is fiercely Provençal and you can reach the centre via Saunerie gate, which displays the Manosque coat of arms – four hands representing each of the mediaeval districts that once made up the early town.

As regards religious heritage, you can visit Saint-Sauveur Church and its beautiful wrought iron bell tower, Notre-Dame-de-Romigier Church with its marble sarcophagus, and the Presentation convent church. The convent chapel was in fact decorated by the artist Jean Carzou between 1984 and 1991 and now features his work *L'Apocalypse des temps modernes*.

For a breathtaking view of the old town, surrounded by the Luberon, Sainte-Victoire and Sainte-Baume, do not forget to climb Mont-d'Or hill 3 kilometres to the north.

Forcalquier, a fountain on a limestone rock

Forcalquier is the first town you come across when leaving Apt – in neighbouring Vaucluse – via the pretty *nationale 100* road.

Formerly independent, almost rebellious, Forcalquier has an interesting history. In the 12th and 13th centuries, it was an independent state and the Bishop of Sisteron even owned a second cathedral here that was known as a cocathedral. Once capital of Haute-Provence, Forcalquier saw four of its children, daughters of the Count of Provence and Forcalquier, become queen. There was Marguerite, wife of Louis IX; Eleanor, wife of Henry III of England; Sanchia, who married Richard of Cornwall, King of the Romans; and Beatrice, wife of Charles of Anjou, King of Naples and Sicily. A fountain in the town displays a plaque in memory of its four queens.

Regarding religious architecture, the town's Notre-Dame-du-Bourguet Cathedral features both Romanesque and Gothic elements and the oldest pipes on its remarkable organ date back to 1629.

Its old town is dotted with small town houses and charming steps, and the generally peaceful *Place Saint-Michel* becomes a hive of activity on market days. If you stroll up the streets of the upper town, you will reach Notre-Dame-de-Provence Chapel and the vestiges of the citadel. The magnificent view here is more than worth the climb up the steep, cobbled streets!

Not just a town, Forcalquier is also an area with a wealth of treasures. So, regardless of when you visit, be sure to make the most of its bright skies, clean air, superb landscapes and delightful hilltop villages.

The old village of **Mane** is full of charm. Its mediaeval citadel, which features a machicolated portal and angle turrets, is the only complete fortification in Haute-Provence that dates from before the 15th century. The **Salagon Priory** has retained its double church since the 12th century and for the last 25 years has been home to the Haute-Provence Ethnological Conservatory. On the inside, it features several exhibitions revealing what life was like in this land, and on the outside it boasts a rich and colourful garden with themed workshops.

Two kilometres away, **Sauvan Castle**, built in 1720, is like a small

Below

Beautiful Notre-Dame-de-Provence Chapel, at the top of Forcalquier Citadel (left). The Salagon Priory, in Mane, is today home to the Haute-Provence Ethnological Conservatory (right).

Above
The surprising "Penitents of Les Mées". These huge grey rocks, shaped by erosion, stretch for a hundred or so metres above the village.

Provençal Versailles and you can even spend a night here!

Not far away, you will find the delightful village of **Dauphin**, the Haute-Provence Observatory in **Saint-Michel**, and the **Oppedette gorge**, a miniature version of the Verdon gorge.

Finally, **Banon**, which is almost closer to Vaucluse than the Alps, is a charming mediaeval village, roughly 1,000 metres above sea level, which boasts the source of Le Calavon, a gently-flowing river. The village will no doubt delight food lovers with its *goûtu*, a small goat's cheese wrapped in four chestnut leaves and decorated with raffia, which has recently been awarded a new AOC quality label.

The middle Durance valley also abounds in beautiful sites, including the pretty villages of **Montfort** and **Les Mées**. The latter is famous for its surprising grey rocks, shaped by erosion and known as the "Penitents of Les Mées". They stretch for a hundred or so metres above the village. In the centre itself, colourful façades and tree-lined streets vie for attention while the nearby **Ganagobie Priory** serves as a glorious reminder of the gift given to Cluny Abbey by the Bishop of Sisteron in the 10th century. Still today, the restored buildings are home to Benedictine monks and you can visit the recently renovated 12th-century church.

Further north, towards the Alps and the source of the Durance River, stands **Sisteron** (or *Segustero* as it was known by the Romans). This pretty town has had an eventful past, experiencing prosperous periods (during the Middle Ages and in the 17th and 18th centuries) and more tragic times (it was attacked by various different armies over the course of its history and suffered heavily during the World War II bombings). It became part of the Kingdom of France in 1483.

Long before you arrive in the town, you will be able to make out

Above
The citadel keeps watch over pretty Sisteron and the impressive Durance Valley. This old town, set between the Alps and Provence, is worth the detour, as is Notre-Dame-des-Pommiers Cathedral.

Below
The charming village of Banon, known by cheese lovers for its soft goat's cheese (left). Not far away stands Ganagobie Priory, given to Cluny Abbey by the Bishop of Sisteron in the 10th century (right).

its beautiful citadel, perched on a rock above the centre and the impressive Durance Valley. Set between Provence and the old Dauphiné province, this citadel, which features elements from various different architectural periods, offers incomparable views of the lower town and far beyond. It was while standing on this impressive mound that King Henry IV of France affirmed that, "It is the most powerful fortress in my kingdom."

Every summer for the last eight decades, the citadel has hosted a first rate festival in its open-air theatre.

Little remains today of Sisteron's ramparts, however, and only three of the original 19 towers are still standing. As for the old town, it is a vast maze of dark and mysterious alleys, arched passageways, steps and small picturesque squares. Its Romanesque-style cathedral, Notre-Dame-des-Pommiers, boasts a delightful sculpted portal and works by Provençal School artists Nicolas Mignard and Van Loo.

The Verdon area

The area around the famous gorge – which is in fact the deepest and most impressive in all Europe – is a patchwork of Alpine and Mediterranean landscapes.

Left page
Every summer, canoes and pedal boats dot the turquoise waters of the Verdon against a backdrop of steep cliffs.

Below
Esparron-de-Verdon – together with Quinson and Sainte-Croix in particular – is one of the reservoirs making up Sainte-Croix Lake.

This lush stretch of land is studded with breathtakingly high cliffs, wild river banks, charming towns and villages, and the superb Sainte-Croix lake with its turquoise waters.

The area is, in fact, home to a Regional Natural Park featuring the gorge, five manmade dams and reservoirs (Castillon, Chaudanne, Sainte-Croix, Quinson and Esparron), rich plant and wildlife, and numerous craftspeople (potters, basket makers, earthenware makers and weavers).

From its source, at the Allos Pass, the Verdon River covers some 175 kilometres before flowing into the Durance. Its territory, which stretches between the *départements* of Alpes-de-Haute-Provence and Var, is definitely worth exploring, if possible in spring or autumn when the climate is mild, the atmosphere quieter and the

Above

The troglodyte Gallo-Roman baths in Gréoux-les-Bains (left). The delightful village of Moustiers-Sainte-Marie owes its fame to the earthenware industry that developed here in the 17th century. A dozen or so craft workshops still make this beautiful earthenware today (right).

colours of the flowers and dormant vegetation, magical.

In the extreme south, your trip begins in the typically Provençal **Gréoux-les-Bains**, reputed for its thermal waters. Its Templar castle was built between the 12th and 18th centuries while its *Maison de Pauline*, a Traditional Folk Art Museum, re-creates a cosy Provençal interior.

Set on the banks of the Verdon, **Quinson** recounts the greatest moments of its prehistoric past through a museum and village.

The old town of **Riez** is home to beautiful buildings and town houses dating from the 16th and 17th centuries. Its baptistery, featuring a baptismal pool surrounded by eight Roman columns with Corinthian capitals, also holds a few Gallo-Roman vestiges.

But the highlight of this trip is undoubtedly the village of Moustiers-Sainte-Marie, built as an amphitheatre overlooking Sainte-Croixaux lake, at the very gates to the gorge. It was founded in 433 by monks and its delightful narrow streets, fountains, washhouses and bridges are sure to fill you with delight. But **Moustiers** in fact owes its fame to its earthenware industry, which emerged in the late 17th century. At the time, the products were said to be "the most beautiful and finest of the kingdom" and there were some seven hundred kilns. The industry later went into decline before being revived in the 1930s, and today a dozen or so craft workshops keep the tradition alive.

Some five hundred pieces of earthenware are exhibited in the village's *Musée de la Faïence*, which demonstrates the excellence of the

Above
Although the bottom of the gorge is a wonderful sight, the top of the river valley offers breathtaking views. Here, *Point Sublime* (left). The village of Castellane, in the shadow of a 180-metre-high cliff (right).

local schools and highlights their different styles. Notre-Dame Church and Notre-Dame de Beauvoir Chapel are also worth the detour. The former stands in the heart of the village while the latter is set high up in the hills. Those of you who attempt the thirty-minute hike to the chapel will be rewarded with a spectacular view.

Finally, the star attraction of the area is of course the gorge itself. The most adventurous among you can explore it on foot, armed with all the necessary equipment, while others can opt for the road route, which also has a few surprises in store. Whether you set out on the D71 in the south or the D952 in the north, you will be astounded by the succession of breathtaking views. Panoramic viewpoints, cliffs, rock faces, narrow gorges and lakes are paraded before your eyes and the scene will be even more amazing if a griffon vulture graces the skies. This two-metre giant, weighing some 10 kilos, has been reintroduced to the area by an association. It joins the numerous other bat and nesting bird species.

Below
Sainte-Croix Lake and its crystal-clear waters, seen from Galetas bridge. The lake's largest beach stands at the foot of this bridge.

Contents

Editor: Christian Ryo
Editorial coordination: Isabelle Rousseau
Graphic design: Editions Ouest-France
graphic studio
Photoengraving: Nord Compo, Villeneuve d'Ascq (59)
Printing: Kapp Lahure in Evreux (27)

Édilarge SA, Rennes
ISBN 978-2-7373-4368-1
Legal deposit: March 2008
Publisher no.: 5551.01.03.03.08
Printed in France
www.editionsouestfrance.fr